BILLY BISCUIT

*The colourful life and times
of Sir William Curtis
1752 - 1829*

J.H. Curtis Dolby and Nick Brazil

Brazil Productions
Oxfordshire, England

© J.H.Curtis Dolby and Nick Brazil 2010

The right of J.H. Curtis Dolby and Nick Brazil to be identified as the authors of this work has been asserted by them by them in accordance with the Copyright, Designs and Patents Act 1998.

Published by Brazil Productions
www.brazilproductions.co.uk.
The Garden Flat, The Mount, Hardwick Road, Whitchurch-on-Thames, Reading Berks RG8 7HW
United Kingdom
Telephone: 0044 (0) 1189841602

First Edition 2010

A catalogue record of this book
is available from The British Library
ISBN 978-184426-921-1

Cover Picture is a detail of *"The Lord Mayor's Show 1791"* by Giovanni Canaletto © Bridgeman Archive 2010

LIMITED FIRST EDITION
TO MARK 215TH ANNIVERSARY
OF SIR WILLIAM CURTIS BT MP

BECOMING LORD MAYOR
OF
LONDON
9th NOVEMBER 1795

CONTENTS

1752 - 1771

Chapter 1 - Wapping 11
Chapter 2 - North America..........................16
Chapter 3 - Formative Years.........................21
Chapter 4 - Married Life................................28
Chapter 5 - Freemasonry...............................33
Chapter 6 - Early Politics...............................38
Chapter 7 - Regency Politics.........................40
Chapter 8 - Drapers Company......................45

1786 - 1795

Chapter 9 - Australia......................................49
Chapter 10 - Wapping Merchants..................62
Chapter 11 - Politics & The 3 Rs....................72
Chapter 12 - The Docks Development 76
Chapter 13 - Banking Beginnings....................81
Chapter 14 - Lord Mayor of London.................86
Chapter 15 - Embarrassing Loan....................93
Chapter 16 - Anne Curtis' Portrait..................96
Chapter 17 - Music Lover..............................101

1809 - 1829

Chapter 18 - The Walcheren Debacle.............105
Chapter 19 - Little P & Bellingham.................109
Chapter 20 - The Czar's Visit........................117
Chapter 21 - Honourable Artillery Co.............125
Chapter 22 - The Sidmouth Affair.................133
Chapter 23 - The Scottish Visit.....................139
Chapter 24 - Gibraltar 1823.........................148
Chapter 25 - Crime & Punishment.................153
Chapter 26 - Royal Ramsgate.......................163

LIST OF ILLUSTRATIONS

Wapping Old Stairs 12
Captain Kydd Inn, Wapping 15
Sailing in High Seas 20
Sea Biscuits 22
Plaistow Lodge 27
Cullands Grove, Southgate 32
Freemasonry Ceremony 34
Life in 18th Century Persia 37
Nadhar Afshah Shah 37
Middlesex Election 1804 40
Drapers Hall, Dining Room 47
Drapers Hall Interiors 48
The Lady Penrhyn 51
Founding Australia 51
Penrhyn Island View and Stamps 57
Whaling frieze 57
View of 18th Century London 66
Curtis' Yacht *Emma* 71
West Indies Trade Network(Map) 72
House of Commons 1793 75
Statue of Robert Milligan 79
Hibbert Gate, West India Docks 79
Map of Wapping & West India Docks 80
Port of London in 18th Century 80
William Curtis & Mrs Coutts 84
Mansion House Dinner Invitation 90
Lord Mayor's Procession 93
Anne Curtis 100
"An Affecting Scene on The Downs " 108
Curtis versus Perceval 110
Sir Francis Burdett's Imprisonment 112
Guildhall Dinner 1814 118
Czar Alexander Ist 121
Statue of Alexander Ist in Taganrog 123
Royal Palace at Taganrog 123
Arab Dhow 124

HAC Infantryman 1803 128
Artillery Division Uniform 1804......................128
HAC Inspection 1803....................................128
Anti Curtis Election Poster 1826.................138
Royal George in Leith Harbour 1822...............143
Royal Procession into Edinburgh 1822..........143
George IV & Wm Curtis in tartan outfits........146
King George kissing Scottish ladies...............146
George IV & Wm Curtis dancing at Levee.......147
Cannon in Gibraltar.......................................150
Trafalgar Cemetery, Gibraltar........................150
Two views of Gibraltar..................................152
Public Hanging at Execution Dock................155
George IV & Mrs Curtis at Ramsgate..............164
"The King's Toothpick"....................................169
Royal Ramsgate..170
Ramsgate Harbour Past & Present.................171

A VOTE OF THANKS

Writing the story of Sir William Curtis or Billy Biscuit as he was affectionately known, has been a long and often complex task. But this task has been made considerably easier by the generous help and encouragement of a number of people. We are particularly indebted to Ken Cozens M.A. Bsc (Hons) of The Greenwich Maritime Institute, Greenwich University for patiently answering the many questions and queries we had about Sir William Curtis. His extensive knowledge of Curtis and the Wapping Merchant Network has been invaluable in fleshing out much of the detail of the Curtis business empire.

Many thanks also go to Tim Curtis who not only made the portrait of Anne Curtis available but also provided information about William Curtis' lifestyle including an eye witness account of his inauguration as Lord Mayor of London.

The important chapter on Australia and The First Fleet was considerably enhanced by the picture and information kindly provided by Bruce Belbin and his mother Mrs Cecily Belbin. Not only have they allowed us to reproduce the fine painting of *The Lady Penrhyn* by the late Phil Belbin, but they also provided us with some fascinating information about their remarkable ancestor Esther Abrahams.

Alexander Mirgorodskiy, Foreign Relations Officer for the City of Taganrog in Southern Russia who generously supplied us with the portrait of Czar Alexander I and a host of pictorial material relating to Taganrog.

We are also very grateful to Philip Margolis of Cozio Publishing in Switzerland who provided some valuable information about Sir William Curtis' musical activities.

We are very grateful to Helen Field, Assistant to Dominic Reid OBE Pageantmaster, The Lord Mayor's Show for the information and historical perspective she supplied for our chapter on Sir William Curtis as Lord Mayor.

Over the years Penelope Fussell, Archivist for The Draper's Company has been a great help and was instrumental in providing the excellent pictures for the Chapter on The Drapers Company.

Jeremy Smith, the Assistant Librarian of The London Metropolitan Archives went to great lengths to ensure we had access to the many excellent images in the Collage collection.

Many thanks also go to Nick Hibbert Steele of Melbourne, Australia who provided valuable information not only about his ancestor George Hibbert but also about the transport logistics of The West Indies Trade.

Rupert Fisher of the College of Heralds also provided important information for the book. We are also grateful to the current Baronet Sir William Curtis and Edward Curtis for furnishing us with details about Billy Biscuit's life.

Heartfelt thanks must go to Roisin Walsh for her patient and meticulous work in proof reading the final manuscript.

J.H. Curtis Dolby and Nick Brazil
Whitchurch-on-Thames, Oxfordshire
April 2010

FOREWORD

Eighteenth Century London provides much scope for historians interested in the making of a city that was to become the premier financial capital of the world. Britain's forging of what was to become a global maritime empire can be largely put down to the enterprise of some remarkable men who were blessed with unique vision and entrepreneurial skills to diversify their operations.

Many of these men laid down the foundations of our now famous institutions such as Lloyd's and the Stock Exchange and developed others such as the Bank of England, to provide unique products and services that offered investments which would make London the international centre for finance and marine insurance.

London's merchants were uniquely placed to develop international trade because of their global networks often utilizing political, business, social and family connections worldwide to a maritime nation. This was made possible because of the far reaching protection supplied by the supremacy of Britain's powerful navy. It was however the important ability to supply this navy that was the mainstay of many London merchants 'bread and butter' trade. Indeed many a fortune was made in victualling the requirements of the Royal Navy.

John Curtis Dolby, a direct descendant of Sir William Curtis and Nick Brazil bring us, for the first time, a fascinating glimpse of the life and times of one of London's most important 18th century figures Sir William Curtis. A man who built upon his family's successful sea biscuit business foundations to become a formidable city figure, an Alderman, MP, a member of the Drapers Company and one of the main contractors who financed government loans.

Researching and putting together much fragmentary family history in this study John and Nick are to be congratulated on producing a fascinating insight into the life and times of Sir William Curtis a truly notable eighteenth century entrepreneur.

Kenneth J. Cozens, M.A.,
Greenwich Maritime Institute Associate,
University of Greenwich

PROLOGUE
JANUARY 1829

Sir William Curtis did not look at all well. A sickly pallor had replaced his normally florid complexion and his breath came in short gasps. This, coupled with his extreme weight made him appear much older than his 77 years. But, in spite of entreaties from his devoted wife Anne, he insisted on going out in his carriage for a ride round his beloved Ramsgate.

The combination of his size and the severe gout that had plagued him for a number years meant that he could not walk even the short distance to his carriage. Instead William had to be carried down the front steps of the house and lifted into the vehicle by two footmen.

As they travelled past the gracious Georgian terraces of the prosperous seaside town, the driver noted that Sir William was unusually quiet. His suspicion that all was not well was confirmed when his master abruptly ordered him back to the house saying he felt out of sorts.

The next day, the Union Jack that always flew from the flag pole outside Cliff House, the Curtis residence above Ramsgate harbour, was at half-mast. It was 18th January 1829 and the life of Sir William, affectionately known as Billy Biscuit, one of Georgian England's most colourful characters had finally come to an end.

CHAPTER ONE
1752
WAPPING

Traditional descriptions of the Thames-side town of Wapping in the 18th Century, usually paint it as a a raucous, violent yet colourful place. The picture that emerges from these accounts is of a maze of narrow, insanitary streets where many legitimate and illegal enterprises plied their trade. Within easy reach of the ship owners and the city merchants, many of these were connected with the seafaring trade.

Respectable businesses like butchers and ship's chandlers rubbed shoulders with whorehouses and taverns and worse. Every night these establishments would disgorge their drunken clientele to vomit into the gutters or the open sewers running down the middle of the streets. Indeed the town boasted a number of famous ancient pubs such as *The Prospect of Whitby, The Bell* and *The Town of Ramsgate.*

The gallows on the foreshore directly in front of the Bell remain to this day. It is said that the bodies of footpads, murderers and pirates were left to hang there until they had been submerged by three tides. But in 21st Century Wapping they serve only to send a shiver down tourists' spines.

In reality, the 17th Century writer John Stow's description of Wapping as a *"continual street or filthy strait passage with alleys of small tenements"* belonged to the narrow waterfront area.

Behind this narrow strip of land there was an altogether more respectable town. This inland area was a magnet for merchants from all over the world. It was here that entrepreneurs with trade connections from Scandinavia to Africa and the Americas established their businesses. This social and commercial environment also attracted a Nottingham baker called Joseph Curtis.

Since the Restoration of the Monarchy under Charles II in 1660, England had undergone a social and economic transformation. Theatres, closed during the grey Puritan rule of Cromwell, were open again and it was possible to enjoy oneself without a furtive glance over the shoulder.

Business in the whole Kingdom was also opening up. Networks of

Wapping Old Stairs by The Town of Ramsgate Pub founded in 1545. The Curtis biscuit bakery and business in Wapping High Street was very close to this inn.
© Nick Brazil 2010

stagecoach routes were established linking all the major English cities. This development was not lost on a Nottingham baker called Joseph Curtis.

As well as being a good baker Joseph Curtis was a shrewd businessman and he soon realised this presented him with an excellent opportunity. He began baking sweet biscuits for the stagecoach passengers who stopped off at Nottingham whilst travelling between London and York. These proved to be an appetising and popular alternative to the variable fare on offer at the inns. They would often be washed down with a hot toddy of brandy and water.

Eventually this flourishing trade diminished as passengers found they could buy fresher and cheaper biscuits at the beginning of their journey in London or York. Joseph Curtis soon realised he had been cut out of the loop. Drastic action was required if his business was to survive.

On his occasional visits to London, Joseph had noted the rapid expansion of the maritime trade between the capital and the rest of the world. Whether it was silk from China or tea from India, large numbers of sailing ships plied their way to and from London.

With ships often away for years all these vessels needed continuing supplies of chandlery and food. Once again the canny baker identified a space in the market waiting to be filled. With the rapid decline of his existing trade, he decided it was time to move his family and business south.

In 1750 Joseph purchased a plot of land 100 yards inland by the Thames-side waters of The Pool of London. Moving his family lock stock and barrel from the Midlands, Curtis re-established his baking business in London.

However, local demand was for plainer fare in the form of rock hard sea biscuits to feed the ships' crews. Within a year virtually every ship travelling to the Mediterranean, Africa or the East Indies had a supply of Curtis biscuits on board.

But there had been one hurdle that nearly scuppered Joseph's business ambitions. To do trade with the merchants of The City of London, he had to swear an oath of loyalty. However, as a Quaker, Joseph was forbidden to swear any oath to King or Country. Forever the pragmatist, Joseph changed his brand of Christianity to the Anglican Church and his rise in business continued.

In 1752 when Joseph's son William was born, the Curtises were well established as pillars of the business community in Wapping. During his childhood nobody would have guessed that young William would amount to very much. Certainly, his headmaster was exasperated by his lack of motivation when it came to his studies. By the time he left school, William was barely educated. This caused him to be the butt of many jokes for the rest of his life. Whilst his spelling may have been poor he was a genius with figures. Nowadays, these symptoms would have been recognised as typical signs of dyslexia.

Like many other great individuals before and after him William Curtis would soon confound his early critics.

The Captain Kydd Pub - typical of the many inns that populated the waterfront in 18th Century Wapping. It is still going strong today.
© Nick Brazil 2010

CHAPTER TWO
1768
GREENLAND AND NOVA SCOTIA

Many young people in their teens become restless and crave adventure. This was as true for sixteen year olds in the 18th century as it is today. William Curtis was no exception to this rule, finding life in Wapping both restricted and claustrophobic.

On countless occasions he would observe the huge vessels gliding down the Thames, past the family biscuit factory with longing and envy. They would be travelling to destinations most people in England could only dream of such as China, the Indies and North America.

After months of relentless badgering, William's father finally agreed for him to travel on a ship bound for Greenland and North America. It is quite likely that the ship was either the *Springfield* or the *Bryan*, both of which were used for the Greenland and North America trade. They were owned by Samuel and John Curteis who had expanded their family brewing business into shipping.

William was taken on either as a Midshipman or a trainee officer and it was a journey that would change his life and fortunes. The ship itself was a merchantman carrying food and material supplies to America. Like many such vessels, there were also a limited number of passengers travelling in both first and second class accommodation.

For the first class passengers, the three week journey would pass in relative comfort. The six cabins reserved for them were spacious, clean and habitable with the luxury of proper bedding aired on deck twice a week. Their food was also good having been carefully stored and cooked by their own steward.

The contrast between this and the lot of the second class or steerage passengers could not have been greater. Their cabins were little more than cupboards into which four people would be crammed, sleeping on beds that were little better than tiered shelves. These cabins were dank, dark and very unhygienic with the constant smell of urine mingling with that of cooking and unwashed bodies.

The steerage passengers would form into groups to collect their rations of rice, flour, sugar and molasses. Unlike those in first class there was no fancy cutlery and they had to provide their own plates. These passengers soon settled into a dreary routine: breakfast at eight in the morning, followed by dinner at noon and supper at six in the evening.

The food for the second class meals was also bland and repetitive consisting of sea biscuits, butter, cheese, tea and porridge for the two daytime meals. At night it would invariably be pork or salt beef finished off with plum duff. On the odd occasion there would also be the treat of a bowl of soup.

Every meal had two ingredients that never varied. The first were those sea biscuits that rapidly degenerated into inedible mush as the sea water seeped into their storage barrels. The second were the weevils that infested the sea biscuits on every ship. Like rats, these horrid little creatures were regarded by passengers and crew as part and parcel of every sea voyage.

The sight of all this horrified William and the memory of those soggy biscuits crawling with weevils never left him. Even at this early stage he began to think that there must be a better way to store such a staple and vital part of a ship's diet.

Lasting three weeks, these voyages to North America were at least much shorter than the eight month marathons to the Far East. Steerage conditions were better as well with proper bedding rather than the sodden straw provided on the ships bound for India.

The steerage passengers were permitted on deck much more often than on the longer journeys. Weather permitting, they would be allowed on deck between seven in the morning and nine at night. It was during this time they could wash and dry their clothes as well as relieving themselves. This latter function meant urinating or emptying their bowels over the side of the ship even in rough seas and lacked both privacy and comfort.

William's voyage to Nova Scotia may have been shorter, but like all the others that followed the same route, was very dangerous. For every ship that made it to North America, many others were lost with all hands in the mountainous seas of the hellish North Atlantic storms. Others sank after hitting icebergs or colliding with whales.

The owners of the ships did not help matters either. Many of the officers on William Curtis' ship were not only illiterate but possessed a minimal knowledge of navigation. If the ship had sunk, few if any of the several hundred passengers or crew would be very lucky to find one of the scarce lifeboats.

Even aboard one of these small craft, chances of survival were very slim since they were often equipped with neither masts, sails nor provisions. Abandoning ship in these treacherous northern waters was not really an option. It would take the massive tragedy of *The Titanic* 145 years later for safety at sea to be finally taken seriously.

The ship's first port of call was Greenland, that huge and mysterious frozen land lying on the edge of the American land mass. Like most ships calling in at the few inuit settlements in Greenland, William's ship traded goods and provisions for seal fur.

From there, they set sail southwards across the grey expanse of The Labrador Sea. Hugging the Canadian shoreline for protection against the cruel Atlantic weather, the ship travelled for another 1000 miles before dropping anchor in the harbour of Halifax, capital of the new British colony of Nova Scotia. Many of the steerage passengers were emigrating to the colony for a better life as planters. However, those in first class were more likely to be entrepreneurs seeking new business opportunities.

Whilst the ship was in port offloading its cargo and re-victualling, William took the opportunity to explore Halifax. Founded barely twenty years before, the port still had the rough and ready look of a frontier town.

With its many saloons and cosmopolitan population it reminded William of Wapping. Then something else reminded him of his home town, the delicious smell of baking. Following his nose he soon discovered a large bakery. When William explained his family background, the owner was delighted to show him around. This establishment was also baking biscuits mainly for the maritime trade.

But that is where any similarity between this and the Curtis business ended. Instead of the biscuits being placed on trays in the oven where they were baked as in his father's factory, here the dough was placed on a large, drum that actually rotated through the oven.

A minute or so later fully cooked biscuits emerged from the other end of the oven. It did not take long for William to recognise the potential for increased profit from this early form of mass production. The whole process was continuous with no time wasted waiting for the biscuits to bake as was the case in the Wapping operation.

By the time his ship set sail for the return journey, William had formulated a plan to introduce the 'Nova Scotia' method of baking into the Wapping factory. This was such a good idea, he was certain his father would jump at the chance.

Being young and inexperienced William had yet to learn that resistance to new ideas could be a very large hurdle indeed. To his disappointment the unimaginative Curtis senior would prove to be no exception to this rule.

One other notable event involving William Curtis occurred on this return voyage. A few miles out of Halifax the sea appeared to take on a life of its own becoming a semi solid writhing mass. In fact the vessel had run into a huge shoal of herring that was so dense it actually slowed her down.

William suggested to the captain that such a rich harvest should not be wasted and they should land at least some of the fish on the ship.

Using spare sails, the ship's crew trawled the herring shoal pouring the fish into the empty holds of the vessel. With this silver torrent went large lumps of floe ice that had been caught in the sails with the fish. This had the added advantage of keeping this unexpected cargo fresh until they reached port.

Sadly, once back in London, the sale of herring did not materialise. It was thwarted by the Clerk of The Fishmonger's Company in The City who would countenance no fish sales except by his own Liverymen. William soon realised the local fishmongers had the whole market well and truly sown up and there was nothing he could do about it. After selling a few pounds to some ferrymen to hawk in The West End and South Bank the rest of the cargo had to be dumped.

Once back in London, William encountered yet further disappointment when his father stubbornly refused to introduce the rolling method of baking biscuits into the Wapping factory. There was no way Joseph Curtis was going to adopt this newfangled way of baking biscuits. What on earth did a bunch of colonials know about manufacturing biscuits anyway?

Despite these two setbacks, William's sea voyage to North America was a life changing event. In the two months since he had left England, William had grown from a callow youth into a confident young man more than ready to take on the world. This would happen much sooner than he expected.

Sailing ship in high seas

CHAPTER THREE
1771
THE MAKING OF BILLY BISCUIT

In 1771, Joseph Curtis set out on a shooting trip in Suffolk with his cousin John Major who was MP for Scarborough. But, he never made it having died of a heart attack en route. His sudden death propelled his two sons William and Timothy to the head of the family business. Such an emergency would test even the most experienced businessman, but for the two Curtis sons it must have seemed a daunting challenge. No doubt, there were those who believed the Curtis baking business would soon fail with two inexperienced people at the helm. But, not for the first time the indomitable Curtis spirit would confound the sceptics.

The two men were very different both in temperament and motivation. Whilst, the elder brother William enjoyed food and drink, he did not let it rule his life. To him, the most important pleasure was developing the biscuit baking business and making money. On the other hand, his younger brother Timothy was far more interested in the fast life of drinking and gaming than in the grubby world of commerce.

As result, Timothy left the running of the family firm to his elder brother. Having a free hand in the factory suited William very well. He lost no time introducing the "Nova Scotia" method of biscuit making into their Wapping factory. This saw a rapid increase in productivity and profits at the bakery. But the problem of protecting the biscuits from the twin ravages of damp and weevil infestation remained.

History does not record exactly when William hit upon an answer to this age old difficulty. Perhaps, it was something he saw on that sea trip which triggered the solution or even a chance remark in a conversation.

But within a short period of taking over the factory, he had his winning idea. With the benefit of hindsight it seems both simple and common sense, but in the eighteenth century it must have been truly revolutionary. He began making biscuit barrels sealed with tar ensuring they were impervious to both sea water and weevils.

These were sold at a premium to those that could afford the luxury of dry sea biscuits free of insects. It would not be long before demand spread so that soon all barrels would be sealed in this way. To reduce waste, a substantial refund was offered on all empty barrels returned to the Wapping factory in good condition. This was sufficient incentive to ensure ships' captains placed a crew member in charge of maintaining the barrels in good shape.

With these two important innovations coupled with William's natural flair for business, Curtis Biscuits became the dominant supplier to the British seafaring trade. It was not long before their barrels of sea biscuits could be found in every ship of the Royal Navy and East India Company. It also earned William his famous nick name:

Billy Biscuit !

18th Century sea biscuits

The world of the Wapping Merchants in 18th century was indeed a tight knit community with its business interests reinforced by many strategic marriages. For example, George Lear an notable sugar refiner and close business associate of William Curtis was also connected by marriage. On 19th November 1803, Curtis' son who was also named William, married Lear's daughter Mary Anne at St Mary's Church, Leyton, Essex.

On 19 July 1766, Godfrey Thornton a merchant with strong Baltic trading connections, had married Jane Godin a member of a powerful Huguenot family. This match connected him by marriage to the influential world of Huguenot bankers and merchants.

Not to be outdone, the West India Merchant George Hibbert married into another important Huguenot family called the Fonneraus. Indeed it is difficult to overstate the importance of the Huguenot influence of the commerce of 18th Century England.

In the years between 1680 and 1760, nearly a quarter of a million Protestant Huguenots fled persecution by the Catholic authorities in France. Their desperation must have been great since King Louis XIV had forbidden Protestants to leave France on pain of death.

Those who were captured and lucky enough to escape execution were sent to be slaves in the French galleys in the Mediterranean. Meanwhile their wives were imprisoned and their children forced into convents.

In total 50,000 of these Huguenots settled in England and became a major force in business, particularly banking. One such man was Peter Isaac Thellusson who arrived in London in 1762.

But it is unlikely this twenty-five year old Frenchman moved to his new country in the same desperate circumstances as many of his fellow Huguenots. Not only had his father Isaac represented the French Court in Geneva, but he was also a successful Parisian merchant in his own right. This, and the fact that he was the London agent for Vendeneyvers who had finance houses in both Amsterdam and Paris indicates that his move was for economic rather than political or religious reasons.

Once in England he soon became naturalised although his assimilation had begun earlier than that. On 6th January 1761 he had married Ann Woodford of Southampton whose father Matthew was a merchant with powerful North American connections. From his business premises in Philpot Lane, City of London, Thellusson worked energetically to build his growing business empire. In 1765 this involved him in The West Indies Trade.

In that year, he invested in the slave ship *Lottery* with John and Anthony Fonblanque, two Huguenot traders also based in the City of London. She was carrying 172 slaves from Africa to work on plantations on the island of Grenada.

From that beginning, Thellusson built up a considerable portfolio of plantation estates in Grenada, Jamaica and the Dutch Colony of Demerara in South America.

Meanwhile, Thellusson was acquiring yet more wealth through speculation on the fledgling London Stock Exchange. He was also forging links within the Wapping Merchant network. These included the shipping partnership of Camden, Calvert and King and the Curtis brothers (see Chapter Ten).

By this time Thellusson was in his forties and was probably allowing his eldest son Peter to take a more prominent role in the business. Peter Isaac Thellusson junior was born in 1761 and although William Curtis was nine years his senior, it was natural they would be drawn together as contemporaries.

Theirs was a lifelong friendship and business partnership with both men's careers often mirroring one another. They worked closely together building up the victualling business that kept The Royal Navy supplied. In fact the Curtis baking business had become so successful that it was using many sub contract bakeries to keep up with demand. Probably the most important of these was Richard Clark who was also in partnership with William Curtis.

As a shrewd businessmen, William Curtis also sought to protect his investments by spreading them over different businesses. One of these enterprises was a gunpowder factory in Wapping. No doubt this was also to supply the ships of The Royal Navy which found itself almost perpetually at war with somebody, usually France.

With huge quantities of inflammable material like sugar and rum stored in such a compact area, Wapping was a prime fire risk. Without a proper fire brigade, when conflagrations broke out, the consequences were often ruinously expensive.

For example, on 1st September 1771, a fire in the sugar refining house of William and John Camden caused £7500 worth of damage. By today's standards that would be approximately half a million pounds.

Understandably, this ever present threat of fire preoccupied the residents of Wapping throughout the 17th and 18th centuries. In July 1673, 200 houses were destroyed in a major fire. Another terrible conflagration occurred in the neighbourhood of Ratcliff in 1794. On that occasion, four hundred and fifty-five houses and thirty six warehouses were destroyed and fourteen hundred people made homeless.

But, as is often the case, one person's disaster is another's opportunity. An ingenious engineer and entrepreneur called John Bristow was not slow in identifying a niche market in this fire disaster business. In 1764, he began manufacturing *"all sorts of engines for extinguishing fires and watering gardens"* in his premises at Bett Street, Ratcliff.

The threat to the goods of Wapping merchants such as Curtis and Thellusson did not only come from fire but also theft. The huge amount of so much valuable merchandise from sugar to coffee and rum often proved irresistible to the criminal fraternity.

In one notable case, a gang including two corrupt customs officials, stole four hundred pounds of raw coffee from *The Three Sisters* a ship owned by the Camden, Calvert and King partnership. In that instance, the perpetrators were caught and went to the gallows. But there must have been many more thefts that went unpunished.

It was these twin dangers of fire and theft that spurred the development of the early insurance businesses. As leading financiers, it was only natural for William Curtis and Peter Thellusson to spearhead this development by founding the forerunners of today's leading insurance companies.

A reminder of these early days of insurance can still be seen on the walls of many old buildings throughout Britain. These are in the form of metal plaques bearing the name and insignia of various insurance or "assurance" companies. If so they would be paid for extinguishing the blaze.

By the late 1780s the Curtis empire had expanded from a baking business to encompass property speculation, assurance, banking and shipping in conjunction with Camden, Calvert and King.

All this was achieved in close partnership with the Huguenots. This business and financial synergy was further enhanced with Peter Thellusson becoming a Director of The Bank of England alongside Curtis' brother Timothy. These important connections would stand Billy Biscuit in good stead when he founded his own bank in 1791. In 1790 both men became Tory MPs with Peter representing the Sussex seat of Midhurst and William representing the City of London.

But unlike William Curtis, neither Peter Thellusson senior or junior would "make old bones". In 1797, Peter Isaac Thellusson senior died at the relatively early age of 60. Sadly, his main legacy for which he would be remembered was not a happy one.

No doubt the will that Thellusson had drawn up was designed to be fair to all members of his large family. Briefly, the £14,000,000 estate was to be divided amongst all his children, grand children and great grandchildren alive at the time of his death. The problem was, that the will was based on the whole estate accumulating in value to the benefit of those surviving heirs.

Unfortunately, a dispute arose between the Thellusson and Woodford families as to who were the actual heirs. This led to a protracted and bitter legal wrangle that was only finally settled in The House of Lords in 1859. As is often the case, the only real winners were the lawyers whose fees must have been astronomical.

The Thellusson Wills Case as it became known, led to a change in probate Law to prevent such an unhappy state of affairs ever reoccurring. It is also thought to have inspired Charles Dickens' novel *Bleak House* that attacked an arcane system of law which encouraged such venal behaviour by the legal profession.

Perhaps it was the stress of his father's legal affairs that led to Peter Thellusson junior dying at the early age of 46. At least he died at home in the magnificent estate of Plaistow Lodge. Today, it houses the Bromley Church of England Primary School.

Although they occurred eleven years apart, the deaths of two such close friends and business associates must have hit Billy Biscuit very hard.

It should be born in mind that early visits from The Grim Reaper were a sadly common feature of Georgian society. This and a lack of contraception, was the reason for having large families. Realistically, at least some of the children in most eighteenth century families were expected to die in infancy.

William and Anne Curtis' family was no exception to this rule. They suffered the tragedy of seeing their first daughter Anna die aged one in 1780. Then five years later, their second son George died aged twenty-one.

But because of this constant presence of death in the background of Georgian life, they would have set aside their grief to concentrate on the business of life.

Plaistow Lodge in Bromley, Kent
Peter Isaac Thellusson's country retreat
Photo © Chris Waring 2010

CHAPTER FOUR
1776 - 1829
A HAPPY MARRIAGE AND A LAVISH LIFESTYLE

In 1776 William Curtis married Anne Constable, the daughter of one of his sea captains at Edmonton. At the time, he was 24 and she was just 19. Since neither of them left any diaries or even letters relating to their married life, what it was like must be down to some inspired guesswork. The one surviving portrait of Anne by L de Longastre aged about forty shows her as an attractive woman (see Chapter 16).

But there are some important clues to the quality and happiness of the Curtis marriage. The fact that it lasted 53 years and they had six children certainly indicates this was a stable and happy relationship. Unlike his easy living friend The Prince of Wales, William Curtis does not appear to have had any mistresses. This would probably not have been the case had the marriage been at all rocky.

So the picture we have is of a devoted couple with Anne as the quiet yet strong power behind the Curtis throne. Throughout her married life, she seemed content to remain in the background whilst her husband basked in the glory of his many City successes, culminating in his inauguration as Lord Mayor of London. She would also have been on hand to provide support and solace to William when he suffered one of his reverses. Such as his forced resignation as Colonel from The Honourable Artillery Company or one of his electoral defeats.

However, it would be a mistake to confuse Anne's apparent modesty with submissiveness. The fact that Anne was indeed her own woman is also shown by her attitude to accepting the peerage offered to William in 1818. Such an honour was not to be turned down lightly.

Indeed, Billy Biscuit was delighted with this and prepared to become Lord Tenterden.

He had decided upon this town in Kent as his Barony because it was where Anne had inherited some land. One can imagine the scene, perhaps over dinner with silver service at their Ramsgate residence of Cliff House when he proudly announced this to Anne. But her reaction was certainly not of delight. Instead, she was furious, announcing that she would not tolerate simply being known as Lady Tenterden. Expecting her to become some sort of marital accessory to Lord Tenterden was a step too far for this quiet yet strong willed woman.

With such close social and business relationships between all the Wapping merchants, life must have been a bit claustrophobic at times. Small wonder that they purchased large properties outside London. These would provide havens of peace where Sir William Curtis and the other merchants could "recharge their batteries".

For his rural retreat, Thellusson senior commissioned the celebrated architect Thomas Leverton to design the magnificent Palladian mansion of Plaistow Lodge. Built in 1780, it was set in spacious parkland. Then in 1790, Thellusson also acquired Brodsworth Hall in Yorkshire.

William Curtis purchased Cullands Grove, a fine Georgian mansion situated in what was then a quiet village called Southgate just outside Enfield in Middlesex. Like Thellusson's house in Bromley, it was a spacious residence set in extensive grounds, but Billy Biscuit discovered it had one significant drawback.

When driving into London, his carriage had to pass through numerous congested villages. His progress to the commercial capital of the empire was often slowed significantly by having to negotiate past anything from a herd of cattle to a hay wain.

These days, most people would have simply moved. Being a rich and important man, Curtis found another solution. He funded the construction of a road that by passed these rural bottlenecks. This early example of the relief road remains as a monument to its originator in the form of Alderman's Hill.

A passionate sailor, William also acquired two yachts. One was a remarkable vessel that he moored on the Thames in The Port of London. Her Dutch name *"Die Jong Vrou Rebecca Maria" (The Young Lady Rebecca Maria)* indicates that she came from the Low Countries. But her provenance was rather more exotic than that because she was a converted dhow. This makes it likely that this 450 ton vessel originally hailed from The Dutch East Indies.

Whilst he used *Rebecca Maria* for ocean and deep sea sailing, Curtis reserved his graceful yacht called *The Emma* for offshore sailing. He moored her in the harbour of the East Kent fishing port of Ramsgate where he had his second home. This was Cliff House, which was built high above the town in the area known as East Cliff. The story of the mutual love affair between Curtis and Ramsgate which lasted his lifetime is described in Chapter twenty-six of this book.

With these two substantial country homes, the Curtis family lived extremely well. How well can be gleaned partly from anecdotal evidence, but also from auction records after the Baronet's death.

James Medcalf was an apprentice shoemaker in Southgate, near Enfield where Cullands Grove was situated. Stories passed down to his descendants tell of a multitude of carriages arriving and departing from Cullands Grove for one of the many great dinner parties held there. On more than one occasion, King George IV was also entertained at the great house.

In his book *Old Southgate,* the author H. W. Newby quotes Medcalf saying that *"not only was the Baronet proud of his cellar but also his kitchen across which a gallery was built so that guests could see how their meal was being prepared."* But the full scale of Billy Biscuit's lavish lifestyle can be gauged from the auction that took place at Cullands Grove after his death. It was conducted by Leifchild and Snelling and beginning *"at eleven o'clock each day on the premises"* on Monday 26th March 1832, took five days to complete.

Among the choice items up for sale were: *"Valuable Paintings of the First Class"* and no less than *"370 dozen cases of choice wines".* Those 4,440 bottles of fine wines included twenty four bottles of Chateau M'Argeaux Claret, *"Two dozen of exceedingly fine East India Madeira arrived in 1816 having been in India five years and bottled in 1822, two dozen of exceeding fine Malaga in pints (a present to the late Baronet in 1815 and stated to be ONE HUNDRED YEARS OLD"* and *"Two dozen uncommonly fine flavoured Port (Boland's Post) vintage 1808"*

One is bound to wonder which lucky members of the auctioneer's staff were deputised to taste this rare stock in the spirit of accuracy. It is a safe bet it was either Mr Leifchild, Mr Snelling or both cloistered in the dusty privacy of their panelled offices.

Three other lots up for auction also gave an insight into the realities and uncertainties of 18th Century life. There were *"Two humane man traps, a wire guard, and sundry useful iron £1 15s 0d."* and *"A capital fire engine with 112 ft of leather hose, three suction pipes and 11 leather buckets... £9 9s 0d."*

It is quite clear that in the 1830s even the wealthiest of landowners had to take care of their own security whether against crime or fire. The total value of 1,114 lots sold at that auction came to £5,532 or about £400,000 by today's values.

No doubt, had he been alive, the old Baronet would have traded all that money not to see his beloved estate scattered to the four winds. The final indignity came in 1840 when a John Donnithorne Taylor bought the Cullands Grove Estate and wasted no time in demolishing the great house.

Today, you would be hard pressed to find any trace of that fine lifestyle except for a few bricks from the old house in various cottages throughout Enfield and a street named Alderman's Hill.

Lady Curtis died in the year following that great auction. By the standards of the time the age of 74 would have been "a good innings". But one can also imagine, the grief and loneliness of living in echoing emptiness of Cliff House without the soul mate of over fifty years may well have hastened her own death. Seeing all the possessions accrued over 53 years of marriage from fine wines to valuable musical instruments, dispersed must also have been a crushing sadness to the old lady. If so, it was a poignant end to a long and successful marriage.

Cullands Grove, Southgate Nr Enfield . Sir William Curtis' country retreat. 1797 picture by Malcolm James Peller.

© City of London, London Metropolitan Archives

CHAPTER FIVE
1777
FREEMASONRY

From a relatively early age, Freemasonry played an important part in William Curtis' adult life. He first joined the Brotherhood in 1777 aged 25 and was initiated as a Freemason in The Dundee Arms Lodge in Red Lyon Street, Wapping. In their book *Wapping 1600 - 1800*, Derek Morris and Ken Cozens record that William Curtis was listed in the Lodge records simply as a *"Gentleman"* by trade and with no official status. His brother Timothy, on the other hand, was already a Master with his trade being listed as *"Biscuit Baker"*.

The picture that emerges from this, is that in the 1770s, William was very much a junior partner both in the family business and in local society. It would be logical that, as a senior member of The Dundee Arms Lodge, Timothy was the one who introduced his brother to Freemasonry. If this was the case, their roles both in business and masonry would be reversed over the next few years.

Since its beginnings in 17th century Scotland, modern Freemasonry has been the subject of a great deal of ill-informed speculation that persists to this day. The most common belief is that Freemasonry is a sinister secret society allied to both criminal and occult forces. Whilst this may make great television drama, it is very far removed from the truth which is much worthier if less exciting.

Freemasonry can best be described as a fraternal and benevolent movement with secrets and private ceremonies. The four main principles that a mason must observe are:

Brotherly Love - showing tolerance and respect for the opinions of others and behaving with kindness and understanding to his fellow creatures.

Relief - that is practising charity and care not only for fellow masons but for society as a whole.

Truth - All freemasons must strive for truth requiring high moral standards in their own lives.

Belief - All masons must confess a belief in a Supreme Being often referred to in Masonic circles as The Great Architect of The Universe.

No doubt the majority of masons both past and present have always been fully signed up to these high principles. Evidence of this can be found in the charitable activities of the Masons.

In England, these include The Royal Masonic Trust for Boys and Girls, The Freemasons' Grand Charity which in 2006, gave grants to people in need totalling over £4.6 million and The Royal Masonic Benevolent Institution - a major provider of high quality services for older people.

But it is unlikely that any members of The Dundee Arms Lodge including the Curtis brothers would have joined purely out of an attachment to Masonic principles and charity. Their main motivation would have been to advance their business and social interests.

18th century Wapping boasted no less than six lodges to which all the most influential local businessmen belonged. As such they were the ideal places to "network" with the good, not so good and the powerful.

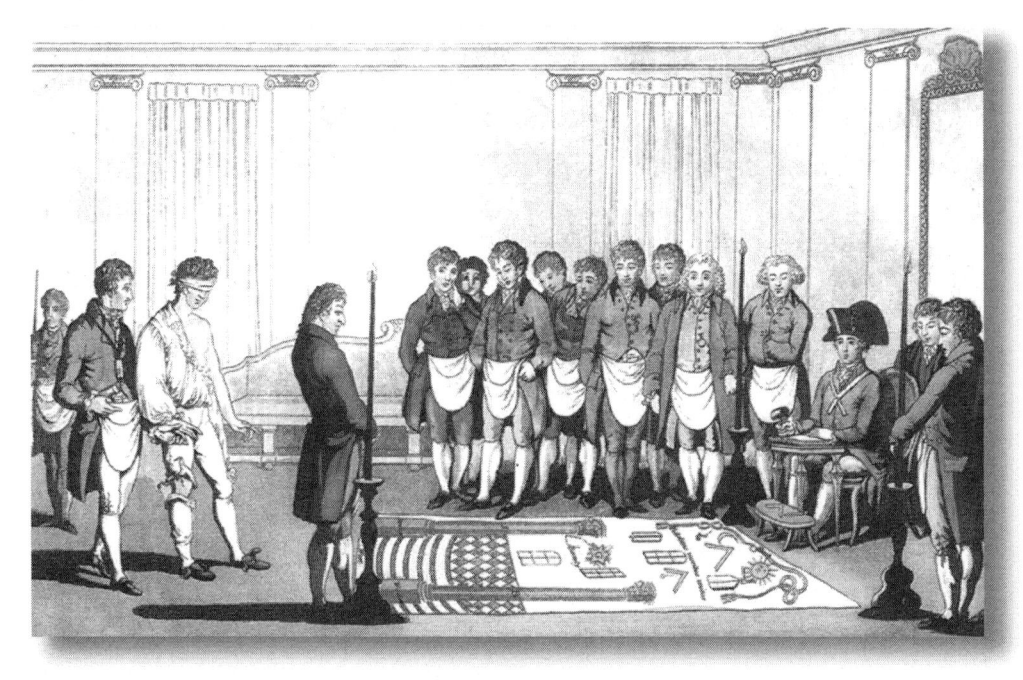

18th Century Freemasonry ceremony in Germany

There were also many gentlemen's dinner clubs that were set up for simply social and business purposes and had nothing to do with the Masons. Some of them even mocked freemasonry by giving themselves names such as *The Ancient Society of Codheads*.

In addition to his Masonic activities, William Curtis certainly enjoyed attending such dinner clubs. One of these, to which both William and his brother James belonged, was organised by William Hickey, the famous diarist.

For Hickey, the prospect of picking up morsels of gossip from the rich and powerful, must have made the cost of entertaining them well worthwhile. After one of these dinners he wrote in his diary:

"I asked James Curtis to officiate, but he pleaded a severe clap which totally incapacitated him from hard drinking."

The fact that Hickey also failed to "dish the dirt" on Billy Biscuit was no doubt due to Curtis' greater shrewdness as well as his monogamous lifestyle. But the exotic history of the masons with its ancient connections to the Middle East and The Knights Templar must also have proved fascinating to a young William Curtis.

According to the late David Lumsden (a friend of the Curtis family) one of his ancestors who was a director of The Honourable East India Company played an important role in William Curtis' early interest in the mystical side of The Brotherhood.

In the late 1760s or early 1770s, when he was still in his teens, William Curtis was introduced to Freemasonry by this Mr Lumsden. The adventurous young man was naturally drawn to such a worldly wise and widely travelled individual.

During their many talks, William listened in fascination as the older man told of the many foreign journeys he made for *'John Company.'* One of these was a diplomatic mission for The Company to The Court of The Nadar Shah of Persia in Isfahan in the late 1730s.

Lumsden explained how Nadar Shah showed considerable tolerance of ancient and pre-Roman religions that still flourished in Persia. He recalled how one religion was dedicated to Mithras and sun worship. He had also been struck by the many signs and symbols in their temples which were similar to those in Freemasonry. These included black and white chequered floors and multiple altars facing South, East and West.

Lumsden spoke wistfully about his stay in Persia and the exciting future it held for "The Company". At that time The East India Company had high hopes of forging a trading and political alliance with the Shah of Persia. These ambitions were brought to an abrupt halt by Nadar's assassination in 1747 followed by a civil war.

This forced the Company to leave Isfahan for the coastal port of Bushir. After a difficult but mainly successful trading relationship with the brother of Karim Khan, the new ruler of Western Persia, the Company eventually quit Persia in 1769.

Whilst Lumsden initially fired William's interest in the esoteric and mystical aspects of Freemasonry, as time went on this would increasingly be at odds with his commercial activities. For it is difficult to see how Curtis squared the principles of Freemasonry with a business that was involved indirectly in the Slave Trade.

Nevertheless, William Curtis' rise in political and business prominence was mirrored by his progression through Freemasonry. In 1790 he was The Honorary Steward of a Lodge that went by the exotic name of The Royal Grand Order of The Modern Jerusalem Sols. The true origins and meaning of this title are a matter of conjecture.

A shorter title which was accorded to Lodges with similar names was *The Jerusalem Sols* or simply *The Sols*. It is probable that '*Jerusalem*' refers to the originators of Masonry, The Knights Templar, who fought in the Crusades to regain that Holy City for Christianity. *The Sols* probably refers to the sun which was a prominent symbol in these lodges.

Curtis' fellow lodge members were a colourful crew ranging from Charles James Fox MP the prominent anti-slavery campaigner to Admiral Hood, a veteran of the American War of Independence and Nelson's mentor.

His great friend, The Prince of Wales was also at the top of Masonry being The Grand Master of England. In 1799, this led to an interesting situation when William Pitt's Government introduced "The Unlawful Societies Act". The prime purpose of this law was to stamp out subversive activity under the guise of Freemasonry. It was particularly targeted at Scotland where the Government feared that the Jacobites were attempting to regroup within some Masonic lodges.

But the fact that the Prince Regent was the leading Mason in England presented the Government with a real conundrum. How could they reasonably ban an organisation whose head was a leading member of the Royal Family?

This thorny problem was circumvented by making all the English lodges exempt from the Act.

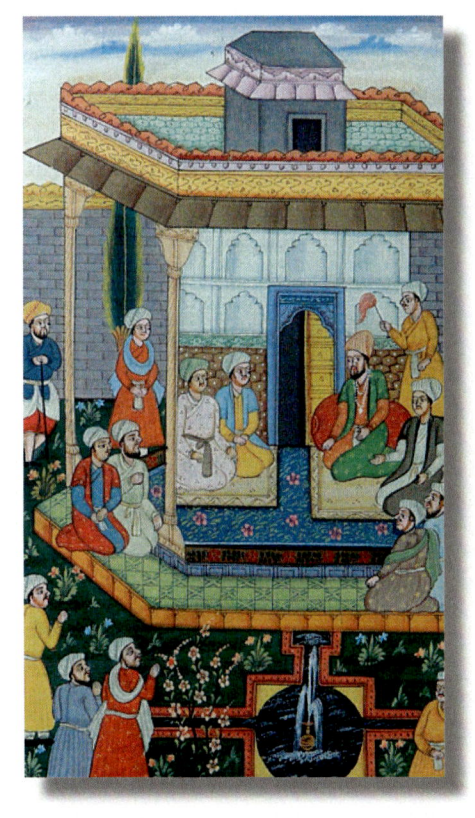

Life in 18th Century Persia

Nadar Afshah Shah

CHAPTER SIX
1780s
A TOUGH TIME AT THE HUSTINGS

In the 1780s Billy Biscuit plunged into the corrupt and rough world of Georgian politics. As *"one of the enterprising set"*, it had long been his ambition to become an MP. Whilst this was mainly to further his growing business interests of the City of London, he was also driven by a strong sense of public duty.

His first foray into the hustings cured him of the idea that the path to Parliament was an easy one. He stood as prospective parliamentary candidate for the seat of Seaford, a very pleasant town on the Sussex coast.

But, as an unknown candidate from London, he floundered badly. The verbal and physical rough and tumble of the campaign came as a rude shock to William who garnered very few votes. It was clear that he had to hone both his oratorical and campaigning skills.

His next opportunity to stand came in 1784 when a vacancy occurred in the Surrey seat of Maldon. At that time, this was a very rural constituency whose populace did not take kindly to *"interlopers from the city"*.

At meetings and in the streets, William Curtis was jostled and verbally abused. He was accused of being *"a refractory London business monopolist"* who knew nothing and cared even less about the needs of this agricultural community. The harsh fact that this accusation was true stung as much as the electoral drubbing he suffered at the hands of Maldon's voters.

Had Curtis been a lesser man, he might have thrown in the towel at this stage and concentrate on his business career. But his resolve was stiffened not only by his wife Anne but also his sister Mary.

The latter had powerful connections with Abingdon which was then in Berkshire. When a parliamentary vacancy occurred there she urged William to stand. Hopefully, this would be third time lucky for Billy Biscuit.

The election occurred at the height of the Napoleonic Wars which was rupturing Britain's trade in agricultural goods such as timber and grain. This, in turn had a grievous effect on the welfare of Abingdon's farming community.

Once again his woeful ignorance of local conditions caused him to falter badly at the hustings. To avoid the humiliation of yet another electoral defeat, he withdrew his candidature before polling day.

It was clear that if Curtis was to have any future in politics, he had to completely rethink his strategy. His friends persuaded him not to waste any more time being pelted with eggs and turnips in unwinnable rural constituencies. They suggested he should campaign on his home ground of London where he was well known and respected.

CHAPTER SEVEN
REGENCY POLITICS - A MURKY WORLD

James Gilray's famous cartoon *"Middlesex Election 1804"* vividly illustrates the complex and often chaotic world of politics in which Curtis was intimately involved. This was one of three highly controversial polls fought by the radical politician Sir Francis Burdett for the Middlesex Parliamentary seat.

As MP for Boroughbridge in Yorkshire, Burdett had already made a name for himself as a radical. Not only had he opposed the Pitt Government's war against France in 1793, but also

Sir William Curtis helps to pull Sir Francis Burdett's *"electoral coach"*. Picture © National Portrait Gallery

denounced the suspension of *Habeus Corpus*. He also wanted greater rights for the people and reform of Parliament. Another of his demands was for an official enquiry into the terrible conditions of Coldbath Fields Prison in London.

Because of these views, Burdett was not popular with the political establishment which regarded him as nothing more than a troublemaker. This thorn in their side had to be ejected from parliament as soon as possible. The opportunity to do this came in the Middlesex election of 1804. Although Burdett had been MP for the seat since winning it in 1802, this result was mysteriously declared void in 1804 necessitating a new election.

Although Sir Francis was defeated, this questionable result was overturned in his favour in 1805. But the hidden hand of the Government intervened again quickly getting this verdict reversed. A disenchanted Burdett who had spent the immense sum of £100,000 on the election declared he would not stand again. For the time being, the powers that be were rid of him, but not for long.

The cartoon makes quite clear where Gilray's sympathies lie and it is certainly not with the status quo. The picture on the flag being carried by the "footman" standing on the rear of Burdett's carriage shows a figure, probably the Prime Minister William Pitt the Younger flogging a distressed and scantily clad Britannia (See below).

This is clearly a reference to Burdett's strong opposition to the trampling of people's rights by the Government and the suspension of *Habeus Corpus*. The flag's slogan *"Governor (name obscured) In All His Glory"* and the banner on the key stating *"No Bastille"* might also refer to the Burdett's criticism of the dreadful conditions in prisons such as Coldbath Fields.

In the cartoon, Gilray also makes a second attack on Sir William Curtis in the form of the dog being crushed under the rear wheel of Burdett's carriage. The name *A (for Alderman) Curtis* is written on its collar.(See below)

There is also a note saying *"A Squiese for the Contractors"* lying amidst coins spilling onto the ground by the animal. This is an attack on Curtis for his 'unhealthily' close financial and business links to the Government. The use of the word *"Contractors"* is probably a specific reference to Camden, Calvert & King, the partnership of Wapping merchants with whom Curtis was intimately involved (Chapter 10). It was also the sort of target Burdett would have in his sights if he became an MP again.

Despite his previous declaration not to stand again, Burdett stood and was elected to the seat of Westminster in 1807. As they feared, he continued to be a radical pain in the neck for the

Government. Even a spell in The Tower of London for breaching Parliamentary privilege over the imprisonment of John Gale Jones, another radical (See Chapter 19) did not cool his ardour.

This was not the only time he faced prison either. In 1820, he was again in hot water with the Government over The Peterloo Massacre. On this occasion his strong attacks on the authorities for their heavy handed response which caused the bloodshed landed him in front of Leicester Assizes. He was prosecuted found guilty of censuring the Government over the incident. The magistrates fined him £1000 (approximately £60,000 in today's values) and he was jailed for three months.

What seems extraordinary to the modern reader is not Burdett's radicalism, but the fact that he was imprisoned twice simply for expressing his opinion as an MP. Were this to happen to an MP today it is unlikely any Government would survive the ensuing rumpus.

Ironically, although Burdett dedicated his life to defending the rights of the common man, it was only great wealth that enabled him to do this. He gained his fortune when he married Sophia Coutts, a member of the banking family. Without the money she brought with her in the form of a dowry, his political career would have been a non starter.

Sophia's father, Thomas Coutts was head of Coutts Bank in the City. This must have brought him into close contact with the Curtis banking interests. As such one might think that the political activities of his son-in-law may have been a severe embarrassment to him.

But, as is so often the case in this period of complex business and political relationships, all may not be as it seems. By reputation, Thomas Coutts was a liberal minded man preferring the company of actors and writers to other bankers. Also, his second wife and Sophia's mother, Elizabeth had started out as a servant in his brother's household. To marry "below his station" must have set a few tongues wagging not that Thomas was the sort of person who would have cared.

So, it is likely that he was naturally sympathetic to Burdett's reformist zeal. Had this not been the case, it is doubtful that Francis' marriage to Sophia with its attendant dowry worth £1,750,000 would have taken place.

However, as far as Curtis, Addington and the Pitt Administration were concerned, Burdett was a fiery radical who should be stopped at every turn. They never quite achieved this and eight years after Curtis' death, Burdett was elected to the seat of North Wiltshire in 1837.

But, to the disappointment of his many followers, he seemed finally to have forsaken his reformist ideals. In these waning years of his political career, Francis sided with his former arch enemies, the Conservatives. After his beloved wife Sophia died on 13th January 1844, Sir Francis Burdett literally pined away, *shuffling off this mortal coil* just ten days later on 23rd January 1844.

CHAPTER EIGHT
1783
BILLY BISCUIT AND THE DRAPERS

The Worshipful Company of Drapers is one of the most prestigious and ancient of the City of London livery companies. Records show that an informal society of drapers existed in 1180. In 1361 it became an official organisation receiving a Royal Charter in 1364. This marked the official foundation of the Company.

What started as a trade organisation for wool and cloth merchants would finally grow into one of the most powerful Companies in the commercial and political life of the City, a position that it still holds today.

Many notable and distinguished personalities have been Members of The Drapers Company. They include Judge Jeffreys, Francis Hawksbee, Curator of Experiments at The Royal Society, Grinling Gibbons the wood carver and sculptor, and Hugh Dalton the Chancellor of the Exchequer in Clement Attlee's Labour Government.

An indicator of The Company's influence in the City is the number of Drapers who have gone on to become Lord Mayor. Since Henry Fitzailwyn, a very early member of the Drapers, became the first Mayor of London no less than a hundred other members have also held that elevated post. In 1783 William Curtis was a rising star in the business and political firmament of The City.

Although he was just thirty-one, it was clear to the decision makers that he was destined for a greater things. He was duly voted in as a member of the Drapers. Not only did this grant him even greater access to the key people in The City but it also gave him a head start in any race to become Lord Mayor.

As a member of The Drapers, Curtis would have rubbed shoulders with the many distinguished personalities of the day. These included First Viscount Keppel who was a distinguished naval officer before entering politics as a Whig MP. But the most celebrated Draper was Lord Nelson, probably the greatest of all British seamen.

However, Curtis' relationship with The Company would not always be one of sweetness and light. As is related elsewhere in this book he was once fined heavily for refusing to stand as Master of The Drapers Company pleading business pressures.

On another occasion he had such a sharp disagreement with the Company that it nearly led to his resignation as an MP. In that instance, Curtis was outraged when he discovered that The Court of The Drapers Company expected him to vote the way they instructed. Refusing to be their lackey, as he saw it, Curtis insisted on voting according to his conscience and his party and not the way The Drapers Company wanted.

When he threatened to resign as MP for London over the matter, it was the Drapers who blinked first. Not only did Curtis keep his seat and integrity, he also fulfilled his ambition to become Lord Mayor. These two incidents must be seen in the context of his membership of The Drapers which lasted for nearly fifty years. Even the most harmonious family would be lucky to escape the odd spat over a similar period of time.

If he could return in the 21st Century, Sir William Curtis would feel equally at home in the opulent surroundings of The Drapers Hall today as he did over two centuries earlier.

What would strike Sir William Curtis is how bright and clear the atmosphere was in all the rooms. The reason for this is that in his day, the magnificent chandeliers would have been lit not by electricity, but hundreds of candles. In Georgian times, virtually every gentleman smoked a pipe. So, no matter how many, the candles would have still struggled to adequately illuminate all the rooms that were pervaded by thick tobacco smoke.

No doubt, Curtis would be pleased to find the Drapers Hall in the same location at Throgmorton Street in the City of London. It is a building the Company has owned since 1543. In that year Thomas Cromwell, Earl of Essex and Chief Minister to King Henry VIII suffered a spectacular and fatal fall from grace.

His error was to botch that irascible King's strategic but disastrous marriage to Anne of Cleves in 1540. Following this, the many powerful enemies Cromwell had made over the years closed in, scenting blood and he was executed on 28th July 1540.

Three years later, The Drapers purchased Cromwell's house

in Throgmorton Street which had been forfeited to the Crown following Cromwell's execution. It has remained their Hall ever since. But over the centuries it has had to be rebuilt twice, due to fire. In 1666 it was completely destroyed in The Great Fire of London and was severely damaged again in 1772.

Miraculously, The Drapers Hall escaped serious damage during the Blitz in World War Two. As the photographs on this and following pages show, The Drapers Hall has not only survived the turbulence, trials and tribulations of the intervening centuries but, like the Company itself, continues to prosper.

The Court Dining Room, Drapers Hall showing the portrait of H.M. Queen Elizabeth II painted by Sergei Pavlenko in 2000.
Photo Courtesy of The Drapers Company

The Drawing Room, Drapers Hall
Photo Courtesy of The Drapers Company

Court Dining Room, Drapers Hall showing The Gobelin Tapestries depicting the Greek legend of Jason and The Golden Fleece. They were purchased by the Company in 1881.
Photo Courtesy of The Drapers Company

CHAPTER NINE
1786 TO 1788
AUSTRALIA

The 1780s were catastrophic for the English Crown. In 1783, her effective defeat in the American War of Independence, deprived England of the thirteen most populous colonies in North America. Apart from the economic loss this entailed it also robbed the British Government of its most important penal settlements.

Then in 1739, an angry British sea captain by the name of Robert Jenkins exhibited one of his severed ears to The House of Commons. Allegedly it had been cut off by Spanish coast guards after they had boarded his ship in the Caribbean. Unbelievably, this sparked a conflict with the Spanish Empire that became known by the surreal title *"The War of Jenkins Ear"*.

But the consequences were far from comic. With British naval ships and merchantmen frequently clashing with Spanish Men O' War, the Caribbean rapidly became a war zone. As a result the plantations of the West Indies were no longer a safe destination for criminals deported from Britain. With the country's prisons rapidly reaching bursting and boiling point another solution had to be found fast.

Fortunately, in 1770, Captain James Cook had claimed a new possession for The Crown. He called it New South Wales, marking the start of of Britain's long association with that vast land which would become known as Australia.

Originally, Cook called the anchorage of his ship Sting Ray Bay because of the large numbers of those fish inhabiting its waters. This was subsequently changed to Botany or Botanist's Bay because of the rich foliage.

After the prolonged and heated "Botany Bay" debate in the House of Commons, it was decided that a penal colony should be set up in Botany Bay. Not only would this solve the problem of prison overcrowding but also provide the British with a toehold on a new land. This was vital in preventing Australia being grabbed by the Spanish and French colonial powers.

As the Banker of the Pitt Government and a Member of

Parliament with extensive merchant shipping interests, Billy Biscuit was delighted by this turn of events. Not only would the Australian Colony provide valuable business transporting the convicts, but to be viable it would also need regular supplies. Sir William could see a glittering future in the new trade with the colony "Down Under".

On 17th May 1787, 11 ships known as The First Fleet under the command of Captain Arthur Phillip set sail from London for the eight month voyage to New South Wales. His instructions were to establish a British colony at Botany Bay on the Southern coast of Australia. Because he had no idea what conditions he would encounter in this new land, Captain Philip asked for experienced farmers and craftsmen as colonists.

But the authorities overrode his request and provided him with 772 mostly illiterate convicts instead. After eight months the fleet arrived at Botany Bay. The fact that only forty of the convicts had died and there had been no serious unrest on the voyage was a major achievement

On 18th January 1788, Captain Phillip, arriving with the First Fleet, stepped ashore from *HMS Sirius* on the Kurnell Peninsula in Botany Bay. Although this name would become synonymous with convicts and transportation it was not actually the first Penal Colony in Australia.

Because the sandy soil was infertile, the British established their first settlement just up the coast in the excellent natural harbour of Sydney Cove. The penal colony established there was named Port Jackson after Sir George Jackson, The Judge Advocate of the British Fleet.

Finance for this expedition was only made possible by the recent establishment of sophisticated marine insurance. This was developed under the auspices of Lloyds of London and helped to lessen the risks of such long voyages. As for the money itself, Sir William Curtis and his colleagues in the city such as Peter Thellusson, made most of it available. These investors became known as "husbands".

But Curtis had a more direct involvement in The First Fleet than most other investors. For his own vessel *The Lady Penrhyn* was one of the 11 ships. Under the Captaincy of its co-owner, William Cropton Severs, she carried a cargo 101 female convicts.

Curtis' ship *The Lady Penrhyn* painted by Phil Belbin Picture courtesy of Mrs Cecily Belbin

"The Founding of Australia"; scene at Sydney Cove, 1788, showing Captain Arthur Phillip, first Governor of New South Wales, proposing a toast to King George III, saluted by the Guard of Marines. Artist: Algernon M.Talmage
© Guildhall Art Gallery, City of London

The prospect of an eight month sea voyage with all its attendant dangers from disease, mutiny or wrecking gave any ship's master more than enough to worry about. But the prospect of transporting over 100 unruly women convicts must have been a total nightmare.

How society regarded these unfortunate women is best summed up in the contemporary *Ballad of Botany Bay*: *"'night-walking strumpets who swarmed in each street, ... whores, pimps and bastards, a large costly crew'.*

But a glance through *The Lady Penrhyn's* records show how truly draconian the law was in the 1780s:

Esther Abrahams convicted of stealing 24 Yards of black silk lace and sentenced to 7 years imprisonment at The Old Bailey on 30th August 1786

Mary Bolton convicted of stealing a quantity of clothing at Shrewsbury and sentenced to death (commuted to 7 years imprisonment) on 12th March 1785.

Elizabeth Leonard convicted of robbery with violence at The Old Bailey on 20 Oct. 1784 and sentenced to death (commuted to 7 years in prison).

Many of these women would have known what the penalty was if they were caught. So the depths of poverty that drove them to risk it and break the law must have been extreme. Another striking fact about this list is that the majority of these convicts had already served half their sentences before being transported. In other words, they were arbitrarily faced with the additional life sentence of banishment without any chance of appeal.

Once at sea the female convicts were at the mercy of the crew who would take their pick of the women. Out of reach of the Laws of England, ships such as *The Lady Penrhyn* effectively became "floating brothels." The most famous of these was *The Lady Juliana*, but *The Lady Penrhyn* had a similar reputation.

It would be wrong to assume that all these women were forced into sex with the crew. Many of those on board were also prostitutes as well as thieves and would have made the most of the situation in which they found themselves.

John White, the Surgeon General of The First Fleet wrote in 1790:

"So predominant was the warmth of their constitutions, or the depravity of their hearts, that the hatches over the places where they were confined could not be suffered to lay off, during the night, without a promiscuous intercourse immediately taking place between them and the seamen ... In some of the ships, the desire of the women to be with the men was so uncontrollable that neither shame nor the fear of punishment could deter them from making their way through the bulkheads to the apartments assigned to the seamen".

Faced with this reality a ship's master had two choices, crack down on this promiscuity and risk mutiny or turn a blind eye. Along with the other masters Captain Severs wisely opted for the second choice.

One of these opportunistic criminals was Esther Abrahams, who had been convicted of stealing those 24 yards of black silk at the Old Bailey in 1786. Although aged only sixteen, Esther gave birth to her baby daughter called Roseanna in Newgate Jail.

When this young Jewish girl boarded *The Lady Penrhyn* with her baby daughter, she could have had no idea how drastically her life would change within a couple of years.

With her black hair, almond eyes and long straight nose, Esther was quite a beauty. Small wonder that she caught the eye of one of her guards, a handsome blond Marine Lieutenant called George Johnston. Seeing in him a good man to protect her daughter and herself during the long and dangerous voyage, she encouraged the lieutenant's advances.

Once they arrived at Sydney Cove, she became Johnston's housekeeper. Although they did not marry until 1814, they were effectively a common law couple from very early on.

Between 1790 and 1808 Esther and George had seven children and Johnston rose to the rank of major in the local militia, The New South Wales Corps. In this capacity he arrested the existing Governor William Bligh during what was known as The Rum Rebellion.

In fact that name is a misnomer which was given to this momentous event many years later. It was actually dreamed up by a Quaker historian called William Hewitt. In his book *A Popular History of Australia*, he seemed keen to blame the rebellion solely on the illegal rum trade. Attributing the whole affair on demon drink would have accorded with his teetotal principles. But all it served to do was trivialise a serious insurrection and disguise its real causes.

Sparked off in January 1808, this was Australia's first and only *coup d'etat*. Essentially, it was about the local military confronting an autocratic governor in a complex struggle for the control of the colony.

Neither side came out of the affair particularly well. The NSW Corps led by Johnston and another officer called Macaulay rebelled against the rule of Captain Bligh. Since he had already faced another mutiny whilst captain of the *Bounty* in 1796, it is fair to assume that Bligh had an unacceptably autocratic style of people management.

On the 26th January 1808, Johnston took the highly risky and controversial step of arresting Bligh. This made Johnston *de facto* Governor of the Colony. For a short period he and Esther were the unofficial First Couple of New South Wales. This came to an end when a new Governor was appointed and Johnston was sent to England to face a court marshall.

This must have been a very worrying time for Esther. By overthrowing the Governor General, Johnston was guilty of rebellion against the Crown which was an act of treason. There was a very real possibility he would face the death penalty.

At his court marshall in 1811, Johnston was found guilty of mutiny. But instead of being hanged he was only cashiered and allowed to return to New South Wales a free man. By any standards this was a remarkably lenient sentence for such an offence and shows that the court had a very low opinion of Bligh as a Governor General.

As matters turned out, Johnston remained a free man until he died peacefully in his bed in 1823 leaving Esther a very wealthy woman. She lived on in an increasingly reclusive and eccentric lifestyle until her death in 1843.

Interestingly, the late Phil Belbin whose atmospheric painting of *The Lady Penrhyn* is included in this book, was the great great grandson of this formidable woman.

As well as the transportation of these unruly convicts, *The Lady Penrhyn* had another secret mission. Captain Severs was under *"confidential owners orders"* to check out the prospects of whaling in the Pacific and treacherous Southern Ocean. For good measure, he was also instructed to investigate the potential of fur trading in the Nootka Sound on the Pacific North West Coast of Canada.

This was a very sensitive mission since the trade in furs with the local Indians in Nootka was the subject of fierce competition between the British and Spanish Governments. In 1789 this led to the Nootka Crisis when the Spanish seized property from John Meares a British resident in the area. For a time it seemed as if the two countries would go to war but this was finally resolved peacefully by the signing of what became known as The Nootka Convention.

Curtis' primary aim in all this was to maximise his profit whilst minimising the risk to himself and his ship. He had already petitioned his friend the Prince Regent to ensure that the Government paid for the transportation of convicts to Australia. This would go a long way to subsidising the whaling and fur trading activities on the return journey to Britain.

There was also another dimension to all this activity by Curtis and the other sea merchants. For a long time they had resented the stranglehold The Honourable East India Company had on Britain's seafaring trade. John Company as it was known colloquially, resisted any incursion into its lucrative marine business, particularly in India and China. Regarding entrepreneurs such as Billy Biscuit as little more than upstarts and freebooters, The Company would go to great lengths to protect its monopoly and curb their activities.

Curtis' cultivation of the North American trade was a way of circumventing John Company's monopoly. Once a ship was on the Pacific coast of America it was a comparatively short step to the lucrative markets of India and China. It was this that would let the genie of competition out of the bottle.

After transporting her cargo of criminals to Port Jackson, *The Lady Penrhyn* then set sail for the Pacific island of Tahiti for re-provisioning. En route she and Captain Severs would be responsible for adding one of the many fascinating footnotes that litter British Colonial history. On 8th August 1788, the ship came upon a huge and isolated atoll measuring 47 miles in circumference. Looking as if it was floating just above the azure expanse of the Pacific, it must have been a beautiful sight..

Indeed, the local name for the island is Tongarava or *"Tonga floating in the clouds."*

It seems unlikely that Severs would have simply passed by the atoll without landing. Apart from natural curiosity, he would want to see if the atoll provided safe anchorage and fresh water as an insurance for future voyages.

Stepping ashore, he and his crew would have discovered a true Pacific paradise with breakers creaming onto pristine sand. Severs named it Penrhyn in honour of his ship and claimed it for Britain.

Today Penrhyn has a population of about two hundred and is the northernmost island of The Cook Islands, which are a self-governing group of fifteen islands in free association with New Zealand. From the air, Penrhyn looks like a giant pearl necklace. No doubt the island owes its shape and existence to the huge subterranean volcano that lies beneath it.

The island's main exports are indeed black pearls. Another "export" are beautiful postage stamps that all bear the name Penrhyn thus linking the Curtis name to this remote part of Polynesia for all time.

After re-provisioning at Tahiti and Tinian, *The Lady Penrhyn* sailed on to China thence to Batavia in The Dutch East Indies. She then returned to England via Cape Town, finally dropping anchor at Gravesend on 12th August 1789. It is a pity that the complete log for this fifteen and a half month voyage is not available since it would make a fascinating book in its own right.

Following this epic voyage, *The Lady Penrhyn* was sold at auction to a London company called Wedderburns. Being the remarkable entrepreneur Curtis was, he and Severs probably sold the ship to upgrade to a bigger and faster vessel. There is no sentiment in business.

Under her new owners, *The Penrhyn* was put on the London to West Indies slaving run which is where she would finally meet her end. In September 1811 whilst sailing to Grenada, she fell foul of a French privateer called *The Duke of Danzig*. Her French captors then burned and scuttled her.

The merchant and shipping partnership of Camden, Calvert and King with whom Curtis was closely involved, played a crucial role in the transportation of convicts. In 1799, CC&K won the tenders

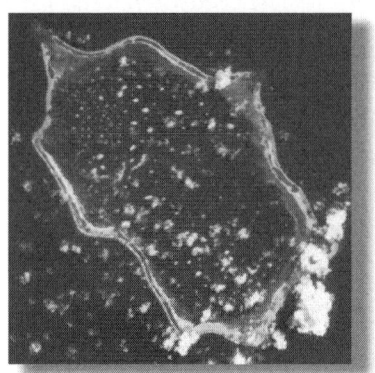

Satellite photograph of
Penrhyn Island,
Cook Islands

A selection of Commemorative Stamps
issued by Penrhyn Island, Northern Cook Islands

A typical 18th Century whaling scene as depicted on the Lydikker
Monument now in The Museum of London Docklands.
© Nick Brazil 2010

for both the Second and Third Fleets transporting convicts out to Australia.

The Second Fleet was made up of four of their ships, *Neptune, Scarborough, Surprise and The Lady Juliana* who weighed in at 401 tons was described at the time as a *"slow sailor."*

A fifth vessel, the 890 ton naval supply ship *HMS Guardian* which was under the command of Lt Edward Riou also accompanied the Second Fleet. On board, she carried a cargo of seeds, plants, farm machinery and livestock destined for the colony of Port Jackson in New South Wales. She also carried a small number of convicts.

After leaving Spithead on 8th September 1789 she arrived in The Cape Colony at the southernmost tip of Africa in November of the same year. This first leg of her voyage to the Cape of Good Hope was an uneventful one that gave no inkling of what was to come. After taking on more supplies she set sail and headed out into the treacherous vastness of The Southern Ocean.

Twelve days later, the lookout spotted a huge iceberg floating some 1300 miles from the Cape. The plants and animals on board had used more potable water than planned, so this seemed an ideal opportunity to replenish the ship's fast dwindling supplies. After closing on the huge iceberg, Riou ordered the crew out in the boats to collect ice.

By the time the boats had returned to *The Guardian* the weather had turned and night was falling. Riou made sail away from that menacing island of ice as fast as possible. But at nine o'clock that evening, the fog which was enveloping the ship was suffused with an unearthly greenish glow. The next moment the crew were confronted by a wall of ice rising high above the rigging and into the night sky. It seemed as if the iceberg had returned to avenge their trespass on her.

In the subsequent collision, *HMS Guardian* was holed but finally managed to escape the deadly clutch of the ice. Nine weeks later, on 21st February 1791, the battered shell of *HMS Guardian* still captained by Riou, arrived back in the Cape. All but a handful of the original complement of crew, family and convicts had survived. To prevent her sinking, Riou beached her but she finally sank on 12th April 1791.

The fateful last voyage of *HMS Guardian* was undoubtedly an epic of courage and endurance, but it is also a vivid illustration of the high price in human suffering that was often paid by 18th century seafarers.

The other four ships all made it safely to Australia but not without incident. Disturbing reports of acute overcrowding and starvation rations amongst the convicts began to surface. This led to the Second fleet having the highest mortality rate in the history of transportation to Australia. Out of a total of 1,026 convicts on board the ships 256 men and 11 women died during the voyage.

In some cases, such as on *The Scarborough*, this was due to inefficiency and neglect. But on other ships the picture was much more sinister. *The Scarborough's* sister ship, *The Neptune*, was commanded by a particularly cruel captain called Donald Traill. Ably assisted by his evil Chief Mate William Ellerington, he delighted in deliberately starving the convicts and keeping them in leg irons for most of the voyage. As a result, scurvy ripped through the emaciated prisoners.

The commander of the guard, Captain William Hill, was so scandalised by the treatment he witnessed he wrote a scathing criticism of the ships' masters:

"The more they can withhold from the unhappy wretches the more provisions they have to dispose of at a foreign market, and the earlier in the voyage they die, the longer they can draw the deceased's allowance to themselves".

But the first ship of The Second Fleet to arrive at Port Jackson in New South Wales gave the residents no inkling of the horror that was to come. This was *The Lady Juliana* the only all female convict ship in The Second Fleet. When she dropped anchor on 6th June 1790 all the convicts seemed in good shape and fine spirits.

The reason for this was mainly because Thomas Edgar, the ship's captain was a particularly good master. A veteran of Captain Cook's voyages, he had learned how to avoid the curse of scurvy. Not only did he ensure the ship's 226 inmates were given adequate rations but also kept the ship thoroughly cleaned and fumigated. As a result there were only five deaths during the whole voyage.

Another reason for the high morale of the convicts can be gleaned from the ship's nickname of *"The Floating Brothel."* All of the men on board had the opportunity to choose a wife from the female convicts, many of whom had been prostitutes in their former lives. No doubt this ensured that the voyage was pretty harmonious. It also ensured that the women had the best possible start to life in their new home.

When the other four vessels arrived at the end of June it was a very different story. The shocked inhabitants of Port Jackson were greeted by a truly grisly spectacle. Skeletal and lice infested convicts dressed in rags staggered ashore whilst those who were too sick to walk were simply flung over the side of the ships. As one contemporary observer wrote at the time, it was *"one of the more horrid spectacles than had ever been witnessed in this country"*

This terrible scandal led to a number of official enquiries which recommended much tighter regulations for the transportation of convicts. No doubt this was a factor in the refusal by most of the "husbands" taking up the offer of future transports.

Apparently £30 per convict for these voyages was not enough. Obviously, the more humane treatment of the deportees did not leave enough profit for these merchants. But neither Curtis nor CC&K were among those who refused and they prospered greatly from the subsequent trade with Australia.

Inexplicably, nobody thought to prosecute either Traill or Ellerington for their wicked mistreatment of the convicts. Eventually a private prosecution was brought against the two men for the murder of a convict and two of the Neptune's crew. But the jury of "twelve good men and true" acquitted both men of all charges after a trial lasting three hours.

Whilst *HMS Guardian* was sailing to her fate in the southern seas, The Third Fleet of nine convict ships mostly owned by the CC&K partnership, was being raised. They were tasked to transport a total of 1,820 English and 200 Irish convicts to New South Wales. Between February and March 1791, the ships of the Third Fleet left England for Australia.

Perhaps the 'husbands' had finally learned from the mistreatment scandals of the Second Fleet. There does not seem to be reports of gross mistreatment on this particular voyage. The fact that 173 male and nine female convicts in eleven ships died en route as opposed to the 267 deaths on the four ships of The Second Fleet seems to bear this out.

Much later, Curtis' son Timothy travelled out to Australia to sound out the possibility of growing flax in New South Wales. This seems a strange choice for a director of the Bank of England. It may have been at the prompting of his father who found Timothy's lack of business knowledge and motivation a severe embarrassment. It had been William who had secured him a post as Director of The Bank of England, so when he proved not to be up to that job, a trip to Australia might have seemed the answer.

Equipped with flax seed from Russia and Ireland Timothy embarked for Australia in 1824. As one of the founder/directors of The Australian Agricultural Company. But his involvement in the venture soon ran aground and Timothy returned to England. He blamed the failure not on himself but on the convicts whom, he said, *"would not do as they were instructed"*.

After his departure, The Australian Agricultural Company fared much better and still thrives today as the country's oldest business. In 2008 its staff numbered 500 managing 24 cattle stations with over half a million head of cattle.

As the story of Esther Abrahams shows, for those convicts who survived the journey and the subsequent rigours of disease and harsh living conditions, transportation to Australia was actually the best break they ever had.

It is also unlikely that Billy Biscuit and the other 'husbands' could have foreseen that these scattered penal settlements would grow into the vibrant modern country that is Australia today.

Definitely a casebook example of The Law of Unintended Consequences

CHAPTER TEN
SLAVERY AND THE WAPPING MERCHANT NETWORK
1790 TO 1829

Leaving the rural constituencies alone was undoubtedly the right move and William Curtis was elected as Tory MP for the City of London in 1790. It would be a seat he would hold successfully for the next twenty-eight years. His entry into Parliament was greatly welcomed by the Conservatives who badly needed a strong figure to stand up to the Whigs whose presence dominated the City at the time.

But although he sat on the benches of the Tory Government of William Pitt the Younger in the House of Commons, Curtis was no party poodle. He would often have sharp disagreements with his parliamentary colleagues and on more than one occasion voted with the Opposition. Easily one of the most contentious issues that caused friction between Curtis and his Party was the repeal of the Test and Corporation Acts.

These archaic pieces of legislation prohibited anyone who was not Church of England from holding public office. Originally brought into force in 1661 and 1673 these acts were primarily designed to shut out Catholics from any position of power and influence.

In effect they cast their net much wider precluding Unitarians, Methodists, Quakers and Jews from partaking in significant areas of the Nation's life. To William Curtis this was an affront to all rules of justice and fairness. In spite of Pitt's opposition to repealing these repressive acts, Curtis sided with the Whig Opposition led by James Fox. This certainly did not endear him with many on the Government benches who already regarded him as a semi-literate upstart from Wapping.

It may seem strange to us that a young reforming Prime Minister like Pitt should resist repealing such repressive legislation as the Test Acts. But his actions have to be viewed in the context of the time.

Memories of the loss of the American Colonies to revolutionary forces in 1776 were still fresh and France had been plunged into a bloody Revolution in 1789. This upheaval soon turned even nastier with Robespierre's Reign of Terror in 1793. In the next twelve months 55,000 French men and women were executed, often on the flimsiest of pretexts.

At this time, the Monarch's role in British politics was far more central than it is today. So, with King George III incapacitated by temporary madness, the threat of revolution spreading to England seemed very real indeed. In the event the Government won the day and the Test Acts were not repealed until 1828, a year before Billy Biscuit's death.

But when it came to slavery, Curtis' attitude and parliamentary activities were much more ambivalent. In one parliamentary speech in 1807 he described slavery as *"an evil that can not be remedied."* He also boasted that while he was an employer of a large number of men he *"never purchased a slave himself or caused his companies to do so"*

From such statements one might deduce that he was resolutely opposed to The Slave Trade. But there is strong evidence to show that the opposite was the case. According to several well placed sources Curtis was not only a leading apologist for the Slave Trade inside Parliament but was an important patron of a group of ship owners heavily involved in transporting slaves.

This partnership was Camden, Calvert and King (CC&K) who had been involved in what was euphemistically called "The West Indies Trade" for many years. As their mentor, Sir William Curtis was also intimately involved with the CC&K partnership and their activities. The main Curtis base and distribution centre at 236 High Street, Wapping was very close to CC&K's headquarters in Red Lyon Street. This was also a stone's throw from the Dundee Arms Freemasonry Lodge also in Red Lyon Street.

As Lodge members, William and Timothy Curtis would often rub shoulders with influential figures in both the CC&K partnership and other major enterprises. These included George Lear, George Hibbert, Fell Parker, Nathaniel Allen, John Stray and Moses Pitt. All these leading players in this network were brought together by common business interests and the shared ambition for ever greater influence and wealth.

William Camden ran a large sugar refining business with his brother which they had inherited from their father. This brought him into contact with the Curtis brothers and their baking business.

Anyone who imported sugar, rum or tobacco at this time had to be involved in slavery. This is because the West Indian plantations relied totally on the slave labour imported from West Africa.

In the 1760s, this mutual interest and involvement in the triangular "West Indies Trade" brought Camden into contact with Captain Anthony Calvert. Unlike Camden and Curtis, Calvert was no "landlubber" but an experienced seaman. In this capacity, he was a regular visitor to the West Indies.

In 1766, he was Master and Owner of *"The Royal Charlotte"* for two voyages transporting slaves to the Caribbean. Then in 1773 he made the acquaintance of Thomas King, another seaman, when they were in joint command of a slave ship called *"The Three Good Friends."*

By the 1770s the three men had formed their highly profitable partnership that soon became inextricably linked to the Curtis business empire. For the rest of the 18th century, this small group of men, led by Curtis, would control one of the largest and most profitable trade networks in the known world.

In his dissertation *"Eighteenth Century London Merchants and the Slave Trade - Networks of Opportunity?"* Ken Cozens of The Greenwich Maritime Institute sums up the group's influence: *"The group were major ship owners engaged in the Slave Trade, who had a diverse number of global operations which received patronage through many of its local connections. The group's main patron, Sir William Curtis used other political and social connections to engage in other enterprises including provisioning African forts and the navy, sugar refining, brewing, shipping, convict transportation, whaling, and later insurance and finance. All based around the partnership's "core" business of slaving which resulted in them being identified as London's premier 18th Century slave traders."*

As well as being a powerful business ally, William Curtis also fought the Group's corner in Parliament. In 1807, he led the Parliamentary Opposition to The Slave Trade Act brought before The House by William Wilberforce, the Yorkshire MP and ardent abolitionist.

In fact this Bill was a compromise reluctantly arrived at by Wilberforce and the Tory Leader William Pitt. Whilst it prohibited the trading of slaves throughout The British Empire it did not abolish slavery itself. Because of this get out clause, the Act had many loopholes. It meant that British Planters could still buy slaves from Spanish or Portuguese traders without fear of prosecution. Nevertheless, Curtis strongly opposed this legislation as James A Rawley explains in his book *London, Metropolis of The Slave Trade*:

"London MPs played a significant role in parliamentary resistance to abolition, executing parliamentary manoeuvres and producing witnesses as well as petitions in the great investigations conducted by the Privy Council, the House of Commons and the House of Lords..... Several merchants, shipowners and manufacturers of London who had 'embarked upon a considerable part of their properties', in the colonies before the order in council was issued now protested the Bill, saying they would apply for a repeal. Sir William Curtis MP for London who presented the protest, declared slavery to be "an evil that could not be remedied."

When viewed in this context, that statement by Curtis is clearly an apologist's attempt to explain slavery as a *necessary* evil rather than a cry for abolition. Slavery was certainly very big business. At its height, ships carried 40,000 slaves a year from Africa to the Caribbean colonies and the Americas. The great American statesman and "champion of the common man" Thomas Jefferson was one notable slave owner and slaves were even used in the construction of The White House.

In the case of CC&K, between 1784 and 1808 they shipped a total of 14,673 slaves from Africa to the Caribbean and the Americas. Of these 8.5% or 1,247 slaves died en route. This business became known as "The Triangular Trade" because the ships of consortia such as CC&K would sail from Britain down to the "Slave Coast" of West Africa. Once there at ports such as Bonny and Whydah, they would barter for slaves with the local chiefs. Goods such as pewter, cooking implements and even weapons were traded for slaves.

One of the great myths that has grown up about the West African Slave Trade was that it somehow flourished without the help of local chiefs and inhabitants. This erroneous belief, often nurtured by film and television, had it that a ship of white slavers would fetch up on some isolated West African beach.

This aquatint view of the Thames in 1800 by J. Swertner shows it in the heyday of The Wapping Merchant network. The building partially obscured by the ship's sail (inset) displays the words "Curtis Baker."

© City of London,
London Metropolitan Archives

    Once there, the crew would tear off into the undergrowth to raid local villages enslaving the inhabitants.
    One look at such an approach reveals it to be a total nonsense. Even assuming the crew were not soon slaughtered for their trespass by the warriors of the local tribes, how would they know where to look for local settlements? In truth, the slavers took the much more pragmatic approach of doing deals with local leaders such as King Gezo of Dahomey.
    In his entertaining but factually accurate novel *"Flash For Freedom*, George Macdonald Fraser relates that, according to Royal Navy estimates Gezo made £60,000 (= £4.25 million in

modern values) a year from trading his subjects for slaves. With a highly disciplined army of 4000 ruthless amazons, he was definitely not a man to be trifled with.

Once the ships were loaded with slaves, they would make the 3000 mile journey westwards to The Caribbean and the Americas. According to Nick Hibbert Steele an author and researcher into the world of George Hibbert, his 18th Century ancestor, the idea that a high proportion of these slaves died en route was also a myth. With a slave costing the equivalent of two year's wages of an English agricultural worker, this would have been a cargo that was too valuable to lose. In fact many slave ships carried surgeons on board to ensure the well being of this cargo of "black ivory".

On arrival in the Caribbean, the slaves would be sold to plantation owners such as George Hibbert and the Milligan and Thellusson family estates. With their cargo discharged, the slave ships would be disinfected with vinegar and burnt sulphur. The idea that these ships returned to Britain with cargoes of sugar and rum is, according to Nick Hibbert Steele also incorrect. Generally these ships would have been considered too unclean, even after being disinfected to carry valuable but vulnerable cargoes such as rum and sugar. The risk of contamination was just too great. Merchant partnerships like CC&K had other ships dedicated to the transportation of sugar, rum, tobacco, cotton and hard woods from the West Indies.

In those days, sugar was transported in large barrels known as hogsheads. Weighing 13.5 cwt, loading and unloading them must have been very gruelling work, particularly in the sweltering heat of the Caribbean. Shipped in 105 gallon casks, rum would also have been a heavy cargo to handle.

Both weather and warfare also made this lucrative trade a highly perilous one. In order to beat the West Indies hurricane season, ships had to leave London by early December to be in the Caribbean for January. They would then have to be gone again before the start of the hurricane season on 1st August. The same went for the slave ships who would have to meet a similar time frame. But they would have the added complication of sailing via West Africa to pick up slaves.

If this were not bad enough, the ships would also have to

run the gauntlet of French and Spanish privateers during the frequent wars between Britain and those two nations. Working on the premise of safety in numbers, these merchantmen would sail in convoys of 150 vessels.

But, no doubt, there were many merchantmen who found themselves outside these narrow time frames. With their departure from the West Indies delayed, perhaps due to quarantine, they would have to brave the dangerous seas and winds of the hurricanes. For some the gamble paid off, but many would have paid the ultimate price and foundered with all hands.

One look at the figures for 1793 to 1799 gives an idea of the scale of losses to British shipping. In that six year period 3,639 ships were captured by enemy forces and 2,967 were sunk. One such ship was *The Cullands Grove* who sank in 1803. The fact that she was named after Sir William Curtis' country estate indicates that it was one of his own ships.

For all these reasons, insuring these ships and their cargoes was a significant cost factor. The worse the condition of a ship the higher the premium. This was also why such "unclean" ships as the slavers had difficulty finding cargoes for their return journeys to Britain. But whatever their condition, all vessels tried to ensure they did not travel back to London or Liverpool empty.

For the merchantmen this was no problem, but the slavers often had to rely on the shadowy trade of "unofficial" cargoes. For some this would mean running contraband into French or Spanish waters. For others, it would be a cargo of rum back to West African ports such as Bonny or Cape Coast Castle. The back bone of all this trade was slavery. So it is little wonder that powerful business forces were ranged against abolitionists such as William Wilberforce.

Without doubt, the energetic activities of the anti-abolition lobby led in Parliament by both Curtis and George Hibbert (who was MP for Seaford)helped to delay the final outlawing of slavery. This only occurred four years after Sir William's death with The Slavery Abolition Act of 1833.

Nevertheless, Sir William Curtis tried to distance himself from being actually directly linked to slavery. In the Museum of London Docklands there is an interesting display that clearly illustrates this. It shows the records of ships and their cargoes travelling on the triangular route between London, the African Slave Coast and the West Indies. Among other names that repeatedly appear as owners of ships transporting cargoes of slaves is Anthony Calvert. But one name that is noticeable by its total absence from this list is that of Sir William Curtis Bt MP.

Nick Hibbert Steele explains this ambivalent attitude thus:

"Curtis by trying to distance himself from the excesses of the Slave Trade had by its very existence enriched himself from it. Without it, and the vast maritime economy that it supported, then the demand for 'sea biscuit' would be severely diminished. It should be remembered that if it was not for the Slave Trade and the taxes paid on the importation of sugar and rum (about 1/3 of the tax revenue of the time) then it could be argued that the British Empire probably would not have existed in any form that we would recognise today."

There is one curious footnote linking Billy Biscuit to this vile trade. In 1822 his yacht *Emma* was allegedly captured by the British authorities off the West Coast of Africa. According to the Registers of British Shipping at the East Kent Archives she was *"condemned as a prize by the Mixed Commission Court of Sierra Leone on 5th day of October 1822 for being engaged in an illicit traffic in slaves."*

As has already been shown, Sir William Curtis was indirectly involved in the 'West Indies Trade' via the CC & K partnership, but it seems odd that he should have allowed his elegant favourite yacht to be directly used in such transportation. Quite apart from the fact that she was too small to carry many slaves, it seems strange that Curtis would have used a vessel so easily traced to him in what was by then an illegal activity.

To seek an informed second opinion on this, the authors asked Ken Cozens what he thought. He was also sceptical:

"I do not think that Curtis's yacht would be at all suitable for any slaving venture (mostly vessels of around 200 tons were used). My theory is it probably was another ship named Emma. Or maybe the ship was sold and it was indeed used in a very small scale slaving venture by its then owner."

In the absence of further information about this episode, the precise truth remains unknown.

Sir William Curtis' yacht *Emma* which he used mainly for offshore sailing seen here off the coast at Ramsgate. It is thought that she was wrongly identified as another brig arrested for suspected slaving in Sierra Leone in 1822
Picture courtesy Tim Curtis

THE WEST INDIES TRADE NETWORK

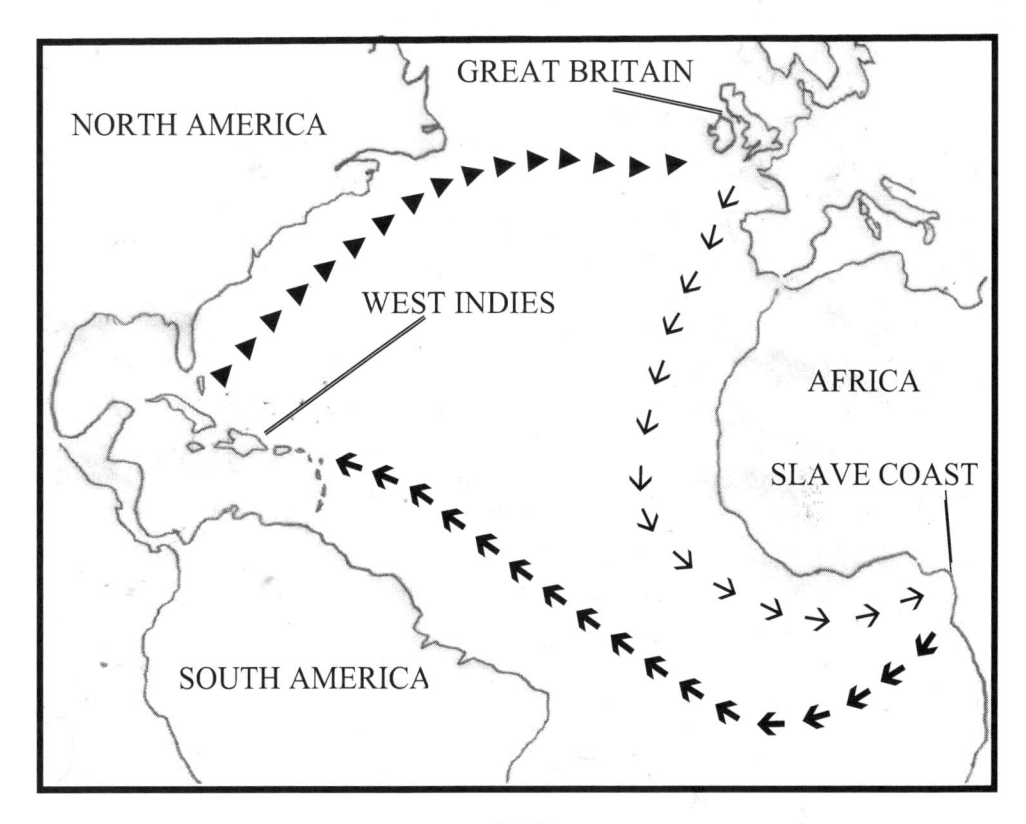

KEY

→ → → →   Ships from London carrying goods to West African "Slave Coast" to barter for slaves and supplies for forts.

◄◄◄◄   These ships then carry cargoes of slaves to sell to work on plantations in The West Indies

► ► ► ►   Dedicated fleet of merchant ships carry cargoes of sugar, rum, cotton, tobacco and hardwood back to British ports such as London, Bristol and Liverpool.

CHAPTER ELEVEN
1790 TO 1795
THE THREE RS

Throughout his time in politics, Sir William Curtis was very active as an MP and a prolific Parliamentary debater. His own comment was that he was a *"bold and plain"* speaker who stuck to the subject being debated. Curtis did not waffle on like some MPs, but made his point as succinctly as possible after which he would sit down immediately.

One famous example of this no nonsense parliamentary style occurred during a debate on the creation of the new Government financed Board Schools. This was an important educational reform that would bring education within the reach of many more of the Nation's children than ever before.

As the debate wore on, some of the better educated *'"Country Members"* began filibustering and insisting it was essential that these schools taught Latin and Greek. At this point Curtis lost all patience and successfully caught the Speaker's eye. Rising to his feet he cut straight to the chase in true Curtis fashion. All pupils at these schools needed, he said in his East End drawl was a good grounding in *"the three Rs, Readin' Ritin' and Rithmatic"*

The statement was greeted with gales of scornful laughter but it was Billy Biscuit who had the last laugh. In spite of this ridicule the House did adopt his *"3 Rs"* approach to teaching.

From then on, reading, writing and arithmetic became the mainstay of state sponsored education for the masses. Some think that Billy Biscuit deliberately misspelt the three words not only as a joke against himself but to make his point as clearly as possible. If so, he achieved his aim beyond his wildest dreams for *"The Three Rs"* is still quoted today as the basis of modern education.

During the Georgian period being an MP was considered an honour and a public duty. As such, Members were unpaid and expected to provide for themselves and their families by means of outside work and business interests. Like many others, Billy Biscuit would work on his many businesses in the morning and attend The House in the afternoon.

In his case, much of his work centred on his business as a successful shipping magnate. This intimate knowledge gave his speeches extra clout when maritime matters were debated in Parliament. Thus he was able to shame a number of south coast harbours, particularly Ramsgate, to reverse the neglect that had blighted their development.

On another occasion, he spoke strongly against the confiscation of vessels caught smuggling. He said this was unfair on the ship's owners who invariably did not know their ships were involved in this illegal activity. As a ship owner himself, he spoke with first hand experience of this problem.

Although there were those members who sniggered at Curtis behind his back, it is fair to say that he was held in high esteem by most MPs on both sides of the House. Proof of this is that the Speaker would frequently entrust him with the job of teller during divisions.

In the 1790s Britain was entangled in a war with France. This led to many blockades and attacks on British shipping preventing her ships from plying their trade with the rest of the the world. As a result, many merchants based in the City of London suffered great hardship. In this matter, Curtis became their champion by supporting Pitt's measures to alleviate this suffering.

At this time the Pitt Government was pushing through measures for a system of naval convoys to protect British merchantmen from attack by French warships and privateers. As a substantial ship owner himself, William Curtis strongly backed this Admiralty plan whose authors candidly admitted that *"much of our trade had suffered from inadequate protection."*

However, one aspect of the plan was disliked by all the ship owners including Curtis. In order to have enough ships for these protective convoys, civilian merchantmen had to be impressed into the naval services. In spite of this clash of interest Billy Biscuit still backed the Prime Minister's plans realising it was the only way British ships could be properly protected.

Because of his high profile in The City of London, he was the natural choice of the Corporation to be their Parliamentary spokesman. But, on more than one occasion, Curtis had to show this was *not* the same as being a simple mouthpiece for one lobby or another. By 1795, he was well established as an independently minded MP who would not be swayed from the right course of action by any amount of pressure.

This came to a head on 3rd December 1795 when the Common Hall of The Guildhall tried to lean on him to do their bidding both as Lord Mayor and MP for London. But Curtis was having none of this. He reiterated that he represented the whole City and not just one narrow interest group. Furthermore, if this was not acceptable to his constituents he would resign immediately.

When push came to shove, it was the members of the Common Hall who backed down and Curtis remained in place as MP and Lord Mayor. They really should have realised he had form in this area of City politics.

House of Commons 1793-94 by Austrian artist A.J. Hickel. In it the Prime Minister is announcing that England has declared war on France. Sir William Curtis can be seen (inset) on the far left of the picture on the second row third from the left with his head turned partially to the left.
Picture © National Portrait Gallery

CHAPTER TWELVE
1795 - 1802
THE DEVELOPMENT OF THE DOCKS

By the late 1790s, London's Docks no longer had the capacity to handle the trade that was flowing into the capital. For example, while the quays had an annual capacity for 32,000 hogsheads of sugar, a single convoy of West Indiamen would bring in 40,000 hogsheads. It was a similar story with coffee and rum leading to cargoes being stacked in the open for long periods of time before the backlog could be cleared. Inevitably this led to wastage due to the weather or theft. One entrepreneur in particular was so angered by these losses that he decided to take action.

This was Robert Milligan who had started life on his family's extensive sugar plantations in Jamaica. Although he could have lived out a luxurious and indolent life as a plantation owner in the Caribbean, that was not his style. A driven man with great energy, he found the colonial life too slow and boring. So, in 1779 aged 33, he left the island for the much more exciting financial world of London.

Once there, he built up a business importing sugar and rum from the West Indies. During this time, he developed close business relationships with many of the Wapping merchants, particularly George Hibbert and William Curtis. It was through Curtis that he extended his reach and influence to the Pitt Government.

By the late 1790s, Milligan became increasingly irritated by the significant losses of cargoes that he and other merchants incurred in the complex of existing warehouses. The two main causes of this were theft and sheer inefficiency which he soon found intolerable. Unlike the other merchants who reluctantly seemed to accept this state of affairs, Milligan developed a plan of action.

One of his closest friends and associates was another merchant with close Jamaican connections. George Hibbert had grown vastly rich from his extensive plantations in Agualta Vale on the island. Based in London, Hibbert's business importing goods such as rum, sugar and hardwood also suffered from the twin ravages of weather and theft. So when Milligan came to him with a plan that would overcome this problem he found a receptive listener in Hibbert. Put quite simply, this plan involved building an entirely new state of the art dock where wholesale theft and waste would become a thing of the past

The two men pulled together a consortium of influential merchants and entrepreneurs to form The West India Dock Company. With his considerable interests in The West Indies Trade through CC&K, William Curtis was also prominent as one of these backers. Without doubt, his close connections with both The Bank of England and the Pitt Government proved extremely helpful in bringing the scheme to fruition.

At the founding ceremony on 12th July 1800, the first stone was laid by Lord Loughborough, the High Chancellor of England. Watching these proceedings with Company Chairman George Hibbert and his Deputy, Robert Milligan was none other than The Prime Minister, William Pitt the Younger.

From that start until completion on Ist September 1802, the development of the West India Dock was driven by the energy of these two remarkable men. As its name suggests, this whole enterprise was designed to cope with the burgeoning triangular trade with the West Indies. Without doubt, Hibbert had a large vested interest in its success, but it was Robert Milligan's original brainchild and he was the one who really got his hands dirty driving the project ahead.

For the next 21 years, the West India Docks had the monopoly of importing rum, coffee and sugar from the Caribbean. But Milligan, the father of the docks would not live to see them reach their zenith. He died in May 1809 aged sixty-three.

Today, visitors to the West India Docks would have great difficulty envisaging the busy seafaring landscape of two centuries ago. In place of the warehouses are futuristic skyscrapers slicing into the grey London sky. These house the City's modern merchant princes and princesses in the form of international bankers and financiers.

Fortunately, in the midst this dazzling 21st century business environment, some timely reminders of the world of Hibbert, Milligan and Curtis have survived. Overlooking the old West India dock is The Hibbert Gate commemorating the start of the enterprise with the following words:

"The West India Import Dock Began 12th July 1800: Opened

for Business 1st September 1802."

On top of the gate is a magnificent scale model of one of the entrepreneur's barques which was named *George Hibbert* after him. As a transporter of sugar, rum, cotton, coffee, and tropical hardwoods from the Caribbean, the real ship would have been a regular visitor to The West India Docks.

But what about Milligan, the originator of the scheme? Shortly after his death in 1809, the Docks company commissioned a statue by Richard Westmacott. On completion it was erected in the docks in 1813 and stood there until 1943.

In that year, the statue was placed in safe storage away from the bombs of The Blitz. Unfortunately, with so much post war reconstruction after 1945, nobody thought to bring it out of storage and Robert Milligan was all but forgotten for the next 54 years.

Then in 1997, his statue was re-erected in its original position in front of one of the few 1802 warehouses that survived the ravages of time, war and redevelopment. Once inside this building, visitors can experience what the world of 18th Century shipping was really like. For it now houses The Museum of London Docklands whose many imaginative exhibits range from vivid audio visual displays to replica streets complete with shops and all the unsavoury smells of that unhygienic period.

The merchant princes of 18th Century England such as Hibbert, Milligan, Curtis and Thellusson were remarkable men who gave much to Britain. But, it should never be forgotten this was achieved at the expense of considerable suffering of the Slave Trade.

The statue of Robert Milligan, founder of The West India Docks in front of The Museum of London Docklands.
© Nick Brazil 2010

The Hibbert Gate commemorating the construction of The West India Docks in 1800-1802 with a replica of *The George Hibbert* merchantman.
©Nick Brazil 2010

MAP OF RIVER THAMES SHOWING LOCATION OF WAPPING AND THE WEST INDIA DOCKS

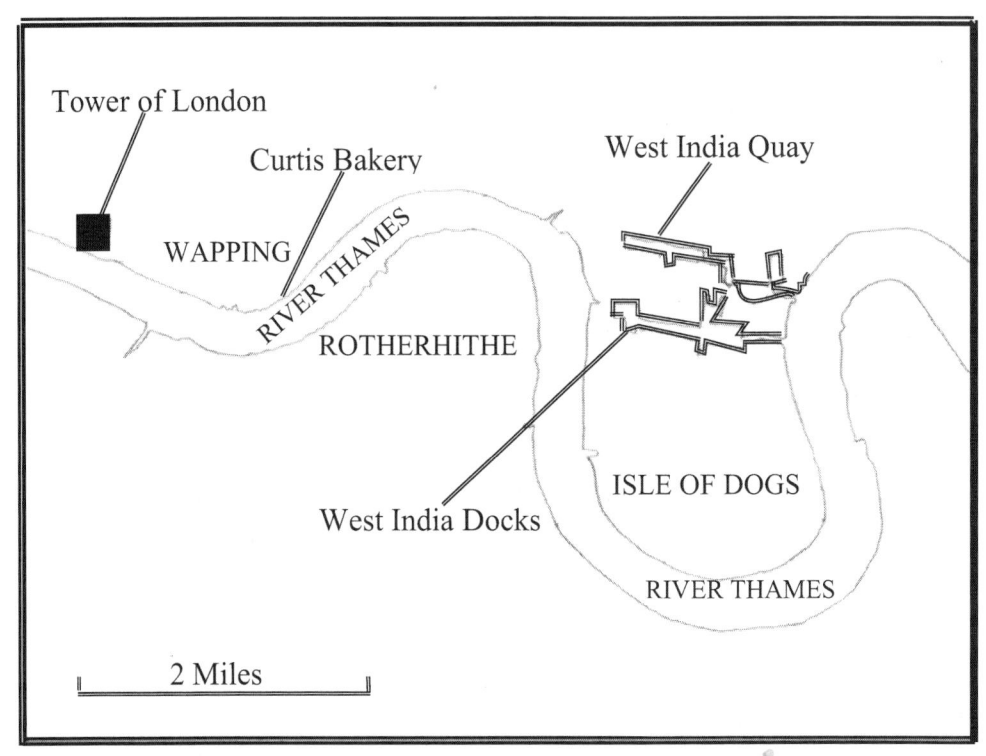

The Port of London in 18th Century

CHAPTER THIRTEEN
1791
THE BEGINNING OF BILLY'S BANK

Successful entrepreneurs are separated from the rest of the population by three important talents. These are an ability to spot a new business opportunity missed by everyone else and then have the energy and imagination to exploit it. This was certainly what gave William Curtis the start to his banking career.

In the 1790s, banking in England was generally long-winded and bureaucratic. This might not have mattered to the Gentlemen of the City who had all the time in the world to conduct their transactions, but for those at the bottom end of the social scale it was a different story.

In the case of the ordinary seamen arriving in London after a long voyage, getting paid was a major operation. Firstly, they had to wait in line with up to hundreds of other men whilst the purser checked their exact time on board from embarkation to disembarkation. Then a chit stating the exact amount owed would be laboriously written out and counter signed by the captain of the ship.

Once ashore, the sailors had to take these promissory notes to the ship's agent in The City. This meant a long walk from the Docks and further tedium whilst they waited on the pleasure of the agents' clerks to pay them out. No doubt, these clerks sought to show their higher social station over these grubby members of the hoi poloi by making this whole process take much longer than necessary. With their hard earned pay finally in their pockets the sailors made their long way back to Wapping and the docks.

This route and procedure would be well known to local criminals who would await their prey like sharks circling a drowning man. How many of these sailors actually completed this journey without being robbed is anybody's guess.

The wages from a long voyage of eight months or so would represent a small fortune to most seaman. Losing it to robbery would have been little short of a disaster. These were the days before the existence of a proper police force, so the chances of catching the thieves and regaining any money were slim indeed.

Many of those who survived these muggings took steps to avoid a repeat performance by having an informal 'banking' arrangement with an onshore acquaintance. These would often be prostitutes or tavern barmaids who would take their man's chit in return for regular payments of money.

Generally, this arrangement worked well, benefiting the local traders and tavern owners where most of this money was spent. But even this method was not entirely risk free. Such women often had connections with local criminals and would arrange to entrap and rob seamen of their chits.

Whenever these ships docked in London, a member of the Curtis Biscuit company would go on board to collect the empty sea biscuit barrels. Payment for these 'empties' was always in gold ensuring that a high percentage were returned in good condition. It was on one of his regular visits to these ships that Billy Biscuit probably saw the opportunity to make money by safeguarding the crew's wages.

Nobody really knows quite how this happened. Perhaps it was a chance remark by a captain or a purser about how many poor seamen were being robbed. Whatever the cause, the effect was to give William Curtis his big idea which was simplicity itself.

He would purchase the crews' payment chits from the ship's captain for an agreed sum in gold less 8 per cent commission. Curtis would then be reimbursed by the ship owners on handing over the chits at their offices. From these modest beginnings, the Curtis banking business was born and grew rapidly.

In 1791 William Curtis was the founding partner of a bank with the clumsy name of Robarts, Curtis, Were, Hornyold, Berwick & Co whose offices were in Cornhill.

It was not long before the bank was lending money to local merchants and even to Royalty. This was in the person of Billy Biscuit's old friend The Prince of Wales who was always strapped for cash. Due to sound management, the bank prospered. In 1795 the bank outgrew its Cornhill offices and moved to 15 Lombard Street where it would remain for over 100 years. Throughout this time, Curtis and his bank worked closely with Thellusson and The Bank of England arranging many large transactions and loans.

It was very much a case of commerce and politics being inextricably intertwined. One transaction that typified this relationship was The Grenada Exchequer Loan. In 1795, the British planters in the Caribbean islands of Grenada and St Vincent faced a two edged crisis that threatened them with ruin. They complained that due to *"ruined crops and war"* they were in danger of defaulting on outstanding bank credits.

Because of their exposure to these loans, this threatened to engulf the London banks in a financial crisis that could destroy not only their viability but that of the vital West Indies Trade.

Not only was Curtis' Bank in the firing line but also the Thellusson family's plantations in The West Indies. For they were one of the leading planter families affected by this with their large estates in Grenada which included the Bacolet Estate. William Curtis and Peter Thellusson devised a strategy to resolve both the planters' and the banks' financial difficulties.

Since both men were influential MPs and supporters of the Pitt Government they were able to successfully lobby the Government to resolve this financial crisis. In 1795 Parliament approved a loan of £5,000,000 in aid to the British banks and merchants who otherwise faced bankruptcy by planters defaulting on their large loans.

No doubt Thellusson as an influential Director of The Bank of England ensured this money was paid to the affected parties as quickly as possible. This crisis certainly has strange echoes of the one that hit British banks in 2008 to 2010. On both occasions a banking collapse threatened the whole economy. Although the sums involved may have been different the threat was exactly the same. *Plus ca change.*

As Curtis' Bank flourished, scores of private banks were established in the wake of his successful venture. But in a haste to make a quick profit, most of these were neither well managed nor well funded. Banking was becoming a bubble just waiting to burst.

This happened with startling suddenness after the Battle of Waterloo. Following the euphoria of victory over the French the nation suffered a huge hangover. Taking the malign form of high inflation and unemployment, it rapidly developed into a full blown financial crisis. Many of those small banks so hastily established in the good times, soon found themselves with insufficient funds to meet their commitments. Inevitably, there was a wave of bank failures leaving customers and investors massively out of pocket.

One of the few survivors of this disaster was Billy Biscuit's bank which would continue to prosper as an independent business until long after William Curtis' death in 1829. Although the old "Robarts Curtis" name of the bank finally disappeared when it amalgamated with Lubbock, Forster & Co in 1860, its Lombard Street premises were still known as "Robarts Office" for many years.

Another survivor was Coutts and Co which had originally been established as Campbells Bank in 1692. It was this bank that eventually took over the Lubbock Bank many years later.

Today, Coutts is known as *"The Queens Bank"* because of its long connection with The Royal Family. It still survives albeit as part of the Royal Bank of Scotland having come through the last banking crisis in 2008-2010.

But all that was still far in the future when Billy Biscuit and his partners surveyed the wreckage of the banking crash of 1815. Forever the shrewd player on the financial scene, Sir William Curtis looked for a way to make his bank even more secure from the financial storms that regularly battered the British economy.

He found it by establishing a Curtis presence within the upper echelons of The Bank of England. By using his considerable influence in the City and the Government, William landed his brother Timothy a directorship on the Board of The Bank. This was yet another cunning move on the chessboard of City life by its most skilful player - Sir Billy Biscuit.

"STOUT AS EVER!"

In this contemporary cartoon of the Regency Period by J. L. Marks, Sir William Curtis is seen handing over a bag of money to Mrs Coutts, the proprietor of Coutts Bank. The stereotypical depiction of a sly Jewish money lender saying *"I will get all dar monish I will play de devil mit tam by cot"* with a foreign accent and Sir William warning Mrs Coutts to *"watch that d....mned jew"* are sadly common racist attitudes of the time. By referring to *"a sleeping partner"* on the notice (bottom right) and a melon being visually compared to Mrs Coutts' ample breasts, the artist seems to be alluding to some form of sexual impropriety between the couple.

On a business level, Curtis' bank Robarts, Curtis and Were enjoyed a close working relationship with Coutts and all the other banks in The City of London. Many years after his death Sir William's bank would be absorbed into Coutts.

Picture © City of London, London Metropolitan Archives

CHAPTER FOURTEEN
1795 TO 1796
BILLY BISCUIT AS LORD MAYOR

By 1794 William Curtis was at the height of his powers. Not only was he very rich and influential in City circles, but as leader of its Tory MPs he was proving to be a loyal and powerful supporter of William Pitt's Government. But all this would pale into insignificance compared to his next great achievement. In 1795 Curtis became Lord Mayor of London which was considered the greatest city on earth at the time.

In the years leading up to his election, Curtis had already established quite a track record in the City's political firmament. Elected as an Alderman in 1785, he became Sheriff for a year in 1788. To be picked by his peers for such a high post was indeed a great honour for this Wapping baker's son.

At this time, Lord Mayors were always drawn from the ranks of *'The Great Twelve'* Livery companies. The successful candidates also had to be active members of one of the City's Masonic lodges. As a leading member of both the Drapers Company and the same Masonic Lodge as The Prince Regent, Curtis was well qualified for this role of undisputed leader of the City of London. It is a position with an unbroken line of 700 occupants stretching back eight centuries.

The significance of the post can be judged by the fact that the Lord Mayor of London is considered second only in importance to the British Sovereign in the eyes of London's power brokers. When it comes to Royalty, The City of London recognises no overlord other than the reigning Monarch.

Prior to 1752 the Lord Mayors would invariably be wealthy City merchants living in their own houses often above their businesses. On election, The Guildhall authorities sent two men to install two bright red posts on either side of the new Lord Mayor's front door indicating where he resided.

Following the Great Fire of London in 1666 it was mooted that the Lord Mayor should have a dedicated residence. But it was not until 1728 that a committee was appointed to select a suitable site, consider plans and, most importantly, work out how to pay for it.

One method of funding was the levying of substantial fines on individuals who refused to serve as a City officer for reasons of either conscience or business. This practice was to continue long after The Mansion House (as the Mayor's residence became known) was completed. None other than Billy Biscuit found this out to his cost when he refused to stand as Master of The Drapers Company pleading business pressures, he was fined a significant sum of money.

Finally, construction of The Mansion House started in 1739. In 1752, Sir Crispin Gascoigne, the Lord Mayor at the time, moved in as its first resident.

Uniquely in The United Kingdom, The Lord Mayor is elected by the liverymen of the Guilds of The City of London. Some of these Guilds are very ancient such as Billy Biscuit's own Drapers Company. Established in 1438, it is number two in seniority.

Right at the other end of the spectrum is The Guild of International Bankers that was only admitted in the first decade of the Twenty First Century, making it 106th in seniority. Nevertheless, their liverymen are equally entitled to vote for the candidates for Lord Mayor.

Interestingly, until the English Civil Wars, Royal Families always chose to live within the Square Mile surrounded by their noblemen and favourites. It might be thought this would often place a member of Royalty in prime position to become Lord Mayor. But in the case of the City fathers, they always rejected any Royal patronage or pressure, preferring to choose one of their own.

Indeed, the list of past Mayors reads like a roll call of the Merchant Princes and their offspring. It is notable that in order of precedence, the Lord Mayor of London is directly after the Sovereign.

Richard the Lionheart's insatiable appetite for fighting The Crusades can be thanked for the establishment of the post of Lord Mayor of London. In total Richard 1st only spent six months of his reign in England which he regarded as his private war chest for fighting his wars in The Holy Land.

In 1189 as a reward for several large loans he took out from

London's aldermen to fight his wars, he granted the City certain rights with a degree of autonomy. This resulted in the creation of the post of Mayor of London with the first incumbent being Henry Fitz-Ailwin de Londonestone. The title Lord Mayor of London was established in 1354 when it was awarded to Thomas Legge during his second term in the post.

In 1379 a Poll Tax was imposed with the level of charging being on a sliding scale according to a person's feudal rank. The fact that London's Lord Mayor was assessed as an earl with his aldermen being regarded as Barons is an indication of the importance of the City's officers. This power and importance was acknowledged over a hundred and sixty years earlier when William Hardel The Lord Mayor in 1215 was the only commoner to sign The Magna Carta.

During his reign in 13th Century, the City's merchants must have upset Edward 1st because he deprived them of their Mayor for 12 years. The most likely reason was a refusal to grant him loans to fight The Crusades. But in spite of such adversities and challenges over the last 800 years, the position and power of The Lord Mayor remains as strong as ever.

Whoever is elected to be Lord Mayor needs to have deep pockets as well as a deep commitment to the job. Whilst The Guildhall provides £2.8 million for the upkeep of The Mansion House, payment of its 60 strong staff and entertainment are the responsibility of the Mayor.

The workload that comes with this important post can also be considerable. So it is small wonder that every decade some aldermen either step down or refuse the honour of this post on grounds of cost to themselves and their families.

Fortunately, for the extremely wealthy Alderman Curtis, money was certainly not a problem. Without doubt, he would have considered the cost of his year in office a small price to pay for the honour and prestige it brought him.

Although the weather on 9th November 1795 was cold and grey, nothing could dampen Billy Biscuit's spirits as he prepared to take up his duties as Lord Mayor. As always it began with the Silent Ceremony at the Liverymen's Common Hall, so called because no speeches are made except for a short declaration by the incoming Mayor.

Then the Mayoral party moved on to the magnificent edifice of The Guildhall. Here Billy Biscuit, the man so often derided by his "betters" received the Mace from Thomas Skinner, the outgoing Lord Mayor.

On the following day as he rode through the capital in the magnificent golden coach, he waved constantly at the passing blur of cheering crowds. It was a glittering start to one of London's greatest occasions, The Lord Mayor's Show. As in earlier years, the Thames was a mass of colourful craft and in the evening the dark sky of the capital was lit up with a sparkling patchwork of fireworks. A contemporary description by *"Aleph"* in *London Old & New* certainly gives a flavour of the event:

"I was about nine years when, from a window on Ludgate Hill, I watched the ponderous Mayor's coach, grand and wide, with six footmen standing on the footboard, rejoiced in bouquets as big as their heads, and canes four feet high, dragged slowly up the hill by a team of beribboned horses, which, as they snorted along, seemed to be fully conscious of the precious freight in the rear.

Cinderella's carriage could never boast so goodly a driver; his three cornered hat was almost hidden by wide gold lace; the flowers in his vest were full blown and jolly, like himself; his horsewhip covered with blue ribbons, rising and falling at intervals, merely for form - such horses were not made to be flogged. The Coaches's box was rather a throne than a seat.

Then, a dozen gorgeous walking footmen on either hand, grave marshallmen, treading gingerly as if they had corns; and City officers in scarlet, playing at soldiers, but looking anything but soldierly; two trumpeters fore and aft blowing an occasional blast..... How that old coach swayed to and fro! With its dignified elderly gentleman and rubicund Lord Mayor rejoicing in countless turtle feeds - for, reader, it was Sir William Curtis !

As the arc of copper, plate glass and enamel crept slowly up the incline, a luckless sweeper-boy (in those days such dwarf lads were forced to climb chimneys) sidled up to one of the fore horses and sought to detach a pink bow from its mane.

The creature felt his honour diminishing and turned to snap at the blackie. The sweep screamed, the horse neighed,the mob shouted and Sir William turned on his pivot cushion to learn what

DINNER AT THE MANSION HOUSE
1796

THE DINNER AT THE MANSION HOVSE
MACRH XXVIII MDCCXCVI
THE RIGHT HON. WILL. CURTIS, LORD MAYOR

This engraved invitation to The Lord Mayor's Dinner at The Mansion House on March 23rd 1796 when William Curtis was Lord Mayor, is by the distinguished Italian engraver Francesco Bartolozzi who moved to London from Venice in 1764.

Soon after his arrival, he became George 111's official engraver on a retainer of £300 per year - worth approximately £21,000 in modern values. This invitation is an excellent example of stipple chalk engraving invented by Bartollozzi. This technique enabled him to reproduce high quality coloured engravings of drawings by artists such as Holbein.

Bartollozzi became a Founder Member of The Royal Academy in 1768.

the noise meant. And thus we were able to gaze at The Lord Mayor's face. In sooth he was a goodly gentleman, burly, and with three fingers of fat on his portly person. Yet every feature evinced kindliness and benevolence of no common order."

The pomp and pageantry of his installation as Lord Mayor brought some light relief to London's citizens in what was, by any standards, a dark and tumultuous year.

It started with the continent in flames and the French Army under the command of General Pichegru taking Amsterdam on January 19th 1795. Then in a dramatic cavalry charge across the frozen waters of the Waddenzee inlet, The French Cavalry then consolidated their gains by capturing the Dutch Fleet at the Friesian port of Texel.

Outnumbered, outgunned and out of luck the Dutch King Willem V and the British army supporting him, beat a hasty retreat across the Channel to England. Meanwhile, in France itself, the Royalists were turning on the Revolutionaries in a welter of bloodshed.

On 7th May 1795 Antoine-Quentin Fouquier-Tinville was tried and executed by guillotine for his role as Chief Prosecutor in *The Great Terror* during the French Revolution. Meanwhile, on June 5th, Royalists killed 700 revolutionaries incarcerated in St Jean Prison, Marseilles.

With much of mainland Europe in turmoil, Britain's vital export trade was severely disrupted sparking an economic meltdown across the nation. A rough idea of how bad things were for the ordinary people was the fact that in Norwich over half the population of 40,000 were on poor relief. As Mayor of the City of London, this economic emergency would test Curtis' entrepreneurial and leadership skills to the hilt.

But in England a crisis of an entirely different sort was just beginning. Involving no bloodshed, it would nevertheless hold the attention of both the public and the ruling classes for many years to come.

In early April 1795 George, The Prince of Wales set eyes on his bride to be for the first time. The atmosphere in the room where this meeting took place was terribly strained. He clearly did not like what he saw and called for a large brandy.

The feelings however were mutual, with his fiancé, Caroline

of Brunswick finding him unattractively obese. Matters did not improve and from then on it was all downhill for the Royal Match. On 8th April 1795, George was drunk throughout their marriage ceremony in The Chapel Royal at St James' Palace, London. It was an inauspicious beginning to a disastrous period of Royal marital relations.

This unhappy marriage of The Prince of Wales to Caroline, the Hanoverian princess was essentially a human tragedy that blighted both their lives. Not only were they totally incompatible, but George was already married to the woman he really loved. This was Mrs Maria Fitzherbert, a widow whom George secretly married in 1785 when she was twenty-nine.

Since she was a Catholic, this created a huge constitutional problem because the marriage was considered invalid under the Royal Marriages Act of 1772.

Designed to prevent members of the Royal Family marrying "undesirable" people, this piece of legislation specifically forbade any members of Royalty marrying a Catholic. In spite of this and with the knowledge that his father was bitterly opposed to his union with Mrs Fitzherbert, George went ahead anyway. Because the ceremony was considered a criminal offence, the wedding took place in some secrecy at Maria's house in Park Lane, Mayfair on 15th December 1785.

For the next ten years, the marriage remained an open secret which was not raised in polite company. Any mention of it sparked ardent denials by George's friends and political allies. On one occasion, the Whig leader, Charles James Fox, declared that any mention of such an "illegal" marriage was a calumny.

Amongst these close allies was The Prince Regent's old friend, Billy Biscuit. He kept no diary so we can not know for sure what Curtis' feelings were about this whole affair. But it is very likely that he closed ranks with Fox and other sympathetic MPs to protect his Royal friend.

Parliament duly voted a huge grant of £161,000 to pay for George's debts plus £60,000 for improvements to Carlton House. As banker for the government and Lord Mayor, Sir William Curtis no doubt played an important role in prizing this out of a reluctant House.

At the end of his tenure as Lord Mayor, Billy Biscuit could

look back with satisfaction. With his steady hand on the tiller, the City had successfully steered through the stormy waters of a national financial crisis and the scandalous marital affairs of an impetuous prince.

The Lord Mayor's Procession in 1761

CHAPTER FIFTEEN
1795
AN EMBARRASSING LOAN

It is fair to say that Curtis' parliamentary career was not entirely trouble free. In 1795, the matter of a £2.5 million loan to the Pitt Government came up for debate. Many members were naturally concerned that the Government was taking on such a vast debt.

This concern was greatly increased when it transpired that the money was being loaned by a Bank owned by one of Pitt's own MPs. The person in question was none other than William Curtis, the Honourable Member for The City and its Lord Mayor. For once Curtis' surefootedness seemed to have deserted him when attempting to deal with this potential scandal.

Firstly, he tried to brazen it out by saying that all the shareholders bar one, a Mr Robarts, were family members and were all quite happy about the loan. He added that he did not *"see why they or he (Mr Robarts) should be corrupted by this matter"*

But then in a complete *volte face*, Curtis admitted that he actually knew nothing of the loan until *"that honest fellow my hairdresser told me of it that morning."* Without doubt, Billy Biscuit had blundered badly.

Once again he was the subject of snide jokes about receiving *"profound and inspired information"* from his barber which he passed on to the Commons in the evening. There were even those who asked if the very authority of the House had not been damaged by this affair.

Although William Curtis survived this embarrassment, some questions about his veracity would dog him from time to time. On one occasion they led to a bitter exchange during a debate on income tax was taking place in the House.

He was on his feet at the time, expressing many reservations about the scheme especially the methods of enforced collection when there was an interjection. This came from an MP called Tierney *'a minor commons gentleman'*. He sarcastically commented that some commercial members of the House were very skilled at tax avoidance.

Stopped in mid flow, Curtis went purple with rage at what he took to be a personal attack on his integrity. He remained standing until The Speaker permitted him to reply to this slur.

Looking directly at the inwardly squirming Tierney, Curtis then reeled off a list of his patriotic loans and prompt payment of his company's taxes. When he had finished The Speaker requested that Tierney withdraw his remarks. Eventually he did but with very bad grace.

CHAPTER SIXTEEN
1794
ANNE CURTIS AND NAPOLEON'S "MASTER SPY"

Since time immemorial, human beings have created images of themselves. Whether they were of their rulers or the ones they loved, these images served as permanent memories in a temporal world.

Georgian society with its great love of portraiture was no exception to this. In the eighteenth century, before the advent of photography, it was to the portraitists that the English upper classes turned for records of themselves and their families. This was the heyday for such painters as Reynolds, Gainsborough and Thomas Lawrence.

But in the case of Wapping merchants such as William and Timothy Curtis, it was not just family members they wanted immortalised on canvas. They also wanted their ships to be celebrated in this way. This led to the rise of a number of fine nautical artists including William J Huggins, Thomas Buttersworth and Francis Holman.

Of these artists, Francis Holman was the closest to the Wapping merchants. Born in Ramsgate in 1729, Holman chose the Wapping area to ply his trade as a marine artist. Unfortunately, only about thirty of his paintings survive, but they are without doubt both beautiful and atmospheric.

Probably the most celebrated of these was a painting he did in 1780 depicting The Battle of Cape St Vincent in moonlight. Another more peaceful work was of the cutter *Fly* running with the wind in full sail against a stormy sky.

In his capacity as the Warden of the Dundee Arms Freemasonry Lodge, Holman knew the Curtis brothers well. This certainly put him in good stead as far as commissions were concerned. Among lodge members who commissioned him was Timothy Curtis for whom Holman did a painting of his merchant ship *The Nottingham.*

Sadly, Holman died at the relatively young age of 55 in 1784. For many years both before and after his death, he remained an underrated and relatively unknown painter. It is only recently that he has been properly recognised as Britain's foremost marine artist.

But William Curtis also liked to have portraits of himself and his family. Probably the best surviving example of this is the portrait of him executed by Sir Thomas Lawrence in 1824. It is now in Her Majesty The Queen's Collection.

This was actually commissioned by Curtis' close friend George IV who was a great patron of Lawrence. It is estimated that the King paid Lawrence a total of £24,500 in commissions. This was a vast sum representing approximately £1,860,000 by today's values.

From a very early age, Lawrence displayed great talent as an artist. The son of a Bristol innkeeper, his father would proudly show his six year old son Thomas' sketches to his customers.

Although he was probably one of the finest portrait painters of the Georgian period, Lawrence did not initially enjoy great financial success until being befriended by the King. His portrait of Sir William Curtis certainly shows all of Lawrence's flair and keen eye for detail.

One of the lesser known artists who also benefited from this portrait boom was a French émigré whom we know simply as L de Longastre. A former colonel in the French gendarmerie, de Longastre spent the last twenty years of his life in England.

Whilst his homeland was immersed in Revolution and terror, he made a very good living creating portraits in pastel of notable members of English society.

Among his many distinguished clients were James Watt, the steam combustion pioneer, Samuel Galton FRS, a member of the Lunar Society and a number of its other members as well as those of The Royal Society. In 1794, he executed a portrait of a Mrs Curtis. The head and shoulders study shows an attractive woman in her late thirties wearing a bonnet with green ribbons.

Nothing is known about the portrait's whereabouts for the next 174 years until November 1968. Then it came up for auction at Sothebys in London where it was bought by Major P P Curtis of Lyndhurst, Hampshire As a direct descendant of Sir William Curtis, he had a personal interest in the picture since he firmly believed that it was a portrait of William Curtis' wife Anne.

Unfortunately, Sothebys were not able to confirm whether this was actually the case, so Major Curtis wrote to Peter Townend the Editor of *Burke's Peerage* for help. Mr Townend replied that:

"I think there is a strong possibility that as the Baronetcy was not created until 1802, the sitter could be the wife of the first Baronet as she was married in 1776 and would presumably be about 40 at the date on the painting."

Sadly, Major Curtis was never able to definitely establish whether the subject was his ancestor before he died. But the circumstantial evidence certainly points to the subject being William Curtis' beloved wife.

Firstly, it would indeed be strange that a devoted husband such as Billy Biscuit did not have a society portrait of his wife. The year 1794 when the picture was painted, could be significant since it was just before Curtis became Lord Mayor. What better reason for such a commission than to have a portrait of the next *'First Lady of London'* ready for hanging in The Mansion House in the following year?

On the other hand, it might just have been a present to mark her birthday. As Mr Townend pointed out, the woman in the portrait was also the age Anne Curtis would have been in 1794.

Whether it was food, musical instruments or paintings, William Curtis always settled for nothing but the best. So, he would also want a picture of his wife to be of the highest quality. This certainly made the talented and fashionable de Longastre the ideal artist to perform this work.

L. de Longastre would also have been very keen to gain a commission from the family of such an eminent individual. As well as opening up the strong possibility of further lucrative commissions from Curtis, L. de Longastre may well have had a darker, hidden motive.

For at the time, he was widely suspected of being a spy for Napoleon. If this was the case, the job of a society portraitist was an ideal cover for collecting sensitive information for his masters in Paris.

It is very intriguing to speculate what valuable titbits of information he may have gleaned from an unwary Anne during her portrait sittings. Any information about William Curtis' dealings with the Government and The Royal Navy would have been "manna from heaven" for the French Government.

In the tradition of all great spy stories Monsieur de Longastre mysteriously dropped out of sight in the late 1790s. Although he is thought to have died in 1799, he seems to have 'returned from the dead' in Birmingham in 1806.

In that year a Matthew Bolton wrote a letter of introduction for an artist called de Longastre to John Wedgewood, son of Josiah, the celebrated porcelain manufacturer. In this letter, Bolton describes de Longastre as *"a French emigrant gentleman"* who was a *"portrait painter in crayons"* by profession.

There is no way of definitely knowing whether that charming portrait of an attractive woman is Anne Curtis, but it seems highly likely. As for de Longastre, he certainly behaved like a master spy.

If he had feared imminent detection as an enemy agent what better way to disappear by "dying" before the English caught and hanged him? Even so, reappearing some years later in the Midlands was still very risky and indicates that he had nerves of steel.

His chameleon like ability to blend in equally well with the French émigré community and the English upper classes, his "faked" death and disappearance all bear the classic hallmarks of the secret agent. But we shall never know for sure, because, like all the best spies he was never caught.

1794 portrait of Mrs Curtis by French émigré
pastellist L. De Longastre
Courtesy Tim Curtis

CHAPTER SEVENTEEN
1795-TO 1829
THE MUSIC LOVER & HIS PRICELESS LEGACY

Sir William Curtis was often savaged by satirical cartoonists like Gilray and Cruikshank or laughed at as a semi literate social climber by his political opponents. But this is very far from the truth. Often pompous and sometimes arrogant, he was nevertheless a shrewd political and business operator.

If he had been the idiot his enemies made him out to be, it is difficult to see how he could have accrued a fortune worth £20 million in today's money. By the same token, if he was such an inept politician, he is unlikely to have risen to be the financial power behind the Government. His City peers also thought enough of Curtis to make him Lord Mayor of London.

But there is yet another side to this complex man that has often been overlooked. Billy Biscuit was not only a great lover of music but also a keen amateur cello player. In this he was by no means a dilettante but treated his musical hobby with the utmost seriousness.

For William Curtis only the best stringed instruments would do. Records held by Cozio Publishing in Switzerland show that, in his life, Billy Biscuit collected some of the world's finest and rarest cellos and violins. According to Philip Margolis of Cozio, he was one of the earliest collectors of these instruments.

His collection included a 16th century cello made by Andrea Amati of Cremona, the inventor of the modern violin. This cello was said to be presented to King Charles IX of France by Pope Pius V. Against all odds it survived the French Revolution to be owned by Billy Biscuit until his death. It now resides in the National Museum of South Dakota.

Both Curtis and his close friend the Prince of Wales were great music lovers. Curtis often took part in concerts with the future King's personal orchestra. It is reported that he and George would sing duets together during these performances. A distinguished musical guest at some of these soirées was the notable Italian violinist and composer Giovanni Battista Viotti.

Between 1791 and 1795, the celebrated Austrian composer

Franz Joseph Haydn paid two long and very successful visits to London. Viotti was guest violinist at some of Haydn's successful concerts organised by the German musician and impresario Johann Peter Salomon. It is tempting to believe that Haydn also accompanied Viotti to some of those Royal soirées and met Sir William. Unfortunately, there is no written evidence of this so it must remain just an intriguing possibility.

Also in Curtis' instrument collection were beautiful violins and cellos made by Amati's sons Antonio and Girolamo and his grandson Nicoli in the 17th Century. One of these was given to Sir William Curtis by his Royal friend after he became King George IV. But the jewels in the crown of Curtis' collection were undoubtedly a viola and violin made by the greatest violin maker of all, Antonio Stradivari.

Had all these instruments remained within the Curtis family after William's death in 1829, his descendants would now have an invaluable collection. Unfortunately, Billy's immediate family did not see it that way. As so often happens with inherited possessions, the instruments were all dispersed and sold off.

Unbelievably, when one of the rarest, the Stradivari viola made in 1696 was put up for auction, it failed to meet the reserve price of 150 guineas. Fortunately, the Spanish Court recognised its worth and it now resides in The Royal Palace Collection in Madrid.

After passing through the hands of a variety of owners, one of Curtis' Stradivari violin was bought in 1924 by Henry Ford, the American auto magnate. It is now on display at The Henry Ford Museum in Dearborn, Michigan.

No doubt Sir William Curtis would have been delighted that most if not all of his beloved instruments have survived intact. He would be equally pleased to know that his Stradivari cello is still being played by its current owners The Los Angeles Philharmonic Orchestra. But the fate it nearly suffered in 2004 would have left him aghast. It is a story more amazing than anything a thriller writer could concoct as this report by John M. Broder in *The New York Times* dateline 19 October 2004 vividly relates: *"The Los Angeles Philharmonic was reunited with its priceless cello on Tuesday, three weeks after a clumsy thief stole it from the porch of the orchestra's principal cellist.*

The cello, slightly damaged, narrowly escaped being turned into a case for compact discs. It is now undergoing repairs and is expected to return to the stage of the Walt Disney Concert Hall in October.

"This is a great day for us," said a beaming Deborah Borda, president of the Los Angeles Philharmonic Association. "The cello and the orchestra are back together."

The instrument, built in the Cremona, Italy, workshop of Antonio Stradivari in 1684, is one of only 60 cellos made by Stradivari still extant and is insured for $3.5 million.

The cello was turned over to the police on Saturday by Melanie Stevens, a 29-year-old nurse who said she found it, in its plastic case, on April 28. Ms. Stevens said she saw it leaning against a dumpster in the Silver Lake neighbourhood, a mile from where it was stolen. She said that she had no idea at the time that the Philharmonic was missing its irreplaceable cello.

Ms Stevens asked her boyfriend, Igal Asseraf, a cabinetmaker, if he could repair the cracks and scratches in the instrument, said her lawyer, Ronald Hoffman.

Mr. Asseraf agreed to try, but said that if he could not fix it he would hinge the top and turn it into a case for compact discs. Ms. Borda said on Tuesday that she reacted with horror when she heard that. "At least it wasn't a planter," she said.

Ms. Stevens stored the cello in a back bedroom and did nothing until she saw a television report 10 days ago about the missing Stradivarius. She contacted a lawyer, who negotiated its surrender on Saturday. A $50,000 reward had been offered for the cello, but it was not clear if Ms. Stevens was eligible for it.

The cello had been taken early on the morning of April 25 from the front porch of Peter Stumpf, leader of the orchestra's cello section. He had inadvertently left the instrument outside, officials said. A security videotape caught the thief riding away on a bicycle and recorded the sound of the bicycle running into trash cans. Ms. Borda, accompanied by the orchestra's stringed instrument conservator, Robert Cauer, went to police headquarters on Monday to identify the cello. Mr. Cauer immediately recognized the instrument, which he has tended for 20 years. He called the damage 'routine'. Mr. Stumpf, mortified, appeared briefly at the news conference announcing the retrieval on Tuesday.

"I'm just incredibly relieved it's been solved and the cello has been returned," he said. *"This has been an enormous weight on me for the last three weeks."*

Priceless in more ways than one!

CHAPTER EIGHTEEN
1809
THE WALCHEREN DEBACLE

At the turn of the eighteenth and nineteenth centuries, Europe was in turmoil. Since 1792, France had been embroiled in wars with other European nations in a variety of coalitions. These included Sweden, Austria and, most notably Great Britain. Then in 1802, the continent experienced peace for the first time in a decade when Britain and France signed The Treaty of Amiens.

But this fragile peace did not last and by the spring of the following year, the two great rivals were again at each other's throats. In 1804, the Swedes joined the British, followed by the Austrians. Once more the corrosive stain of war was spreading across the continent.

In August 1805, the roads, lanes and fields of France were filled with the blue masses of Napoleon's Grande Armée. 200,000 men advanced in great secrecy across a front of 160 miles. In October 1805 they stormed across the Rhine and into Bavaria. This bold and early example of blitzkrieg finally netted 23,000 Austrian soldiers under General Mack. Surrounded and outnumbered by French forces the Austrians surrendered at the Bavarian City of Ulm.

By 1809 the French seemed invincible. In a succession of bold campaigns, their forces steadily increased the size of Napoleon's Empire. In Portugal and Spain they were fighting the British under Wellington. In the North they occupied a large chunk of Prussia and the Netherlands. Britain had now been continuously at war with Napoleon for six years and was desperate to turn the tide.

On 30th July 1809, a large British expeditionary force sailed across The North Sea to the Dutch island of Walcheren. On board the ships were 40,000 soldiers, 15,000 horses, artillery pieces and two siege trains. Although it was a far larger force than Wellington's army in Iberia it would prove substantially less successful.

Amongst this extensive convoy of large ships plying across

the leaden waters of the North Sea could be seen the substantial shape of the ocean going yacht *Die Jong Vrow Rebecca Maria*. On board was her owner Sir William Curtis who was carrying *"delicate refreshments of all kinds to the military and naval commanders and the principal officers"*.

When the British captured the port of Flushing on 15th August 1809, the awful truth dawned that the French had flown the nest. With the Fleet now beyond their reach in Antwerp, the British force was stuck on this swampy island with nowhere to go. But worse was yet to come.

Warfare in this period was an extremely bloody business. For example, The Battle of Eylau in February 1807 left 50,000 French and Russian casualties. But in spite of this grisly reality, war was regarded as a gentlemanly pursuit amongst Europe's nobility. It was not unknown for the local gentry to turn out in their carriages to observe the slaughter of battle from the safety of a distant hillside. To fortify themselves, they would bring picnic hampers complete with servants to wait on their every whim.

No doubt this is how Billy Biscuit regarded The Walcheren Expedition. It is also quite possible that he felt a duty to 'keep an eye' on John Pitt, Second Earl of Chatham who was leading the expedition. Chatham was the brother of one of Curtis' close friends, William Pitt the Younger who had died in 1806.

Perhaps Curtis was honouring the memory of his late friend by looking out for his sibling or simply wanting a bit of excitement. Whatever the reason, he was about to witness the start of one of Britain's great military disasters.

From the outset the Walcheren Expedition was badly planned and executed. Extremely poor military intelligence meant that the British did not know the French fleet had been moved from Flushing to the safety of Antwerp before they even arrived on Walcheren Island.

Similarly, they were also unaware that their Austrian allies had surrendered to the French after the Battle of Wagram earlier in the summer. Since one of the main reasons for this British expedition was to take French pressure off the Austrians, the whole enterprise was doomed before it began.

Throughout the four month campaign only one hundred and

six British soldiers died in action against the French. But a much more insidious enemy would soon kill another 4000 men. What at the time was called *Walcheren Fever* was actually malaria and it was rife in the island's swamplands. It ripped through the British forces leaving ten per cent of them dead and another 12000 unfit for duty.

When the British finally left Walcheren Island in December 1809, the whole debacle had cost £8,000,000 - £320 million in today's values. This futile venture had been a costly debacle in terms of money and human lives.

It is unclear whether William Curtis stayed for the whole campaign, but it seems unlikely. With his many commitments in the City, business and politics, he probably returned to England after not more than a few days. It is also possible that the harrowing spectacle of so many troops dying of *Walcheren Fever* might have prompted his early departure.

AN AFFECTING SCENE IN THE DOWNS

This Cruikshank cartoon shows The Foreign Secretary Castlereagh bidding a tearful farewell to Billy Biscuit whilst the rest of the fleet waits to set sail on The Walcheren Expedition. This probably alludes to the fact that Castlereagh tried to dissuade Curtis from going on what he thought was a dangerous military expedition.

As is often the case in contemporary cartoons, Sir William Curtis is pictured with a turtle around his neck. This is an allusion to his favourite dish of turtle soup. His love of food is also lampooned by the varieties of vegetables and sausages hanging from the yacht and a cooking pot sitting on a table. As is often the case Curtis' prominent nose is exaggerated..

This cartoon is accompanied by a satirical poem titled *"An Affecting Scene in the Downs"* lampooning Castlereagh, Curtis and the whole Expedition. The contemporary press thought little of the Walcheren venture at its outset but were even more scathing about its disastrous outcome.

The Downs in the title refers to an area of shallows off the south coast and not the rolling hills inland.

Cruikshank cartoon © City of London, London Metropolitan Archives

CHAPTER NINETEEN
"LITTLE P" AND JOHN BELLINGHAM
1809 - 1812

The repercussions from the Walcheren Disaster reverberated through the British body politic and for a time threatened to bring down the Government. The fact that it did not was largely due to the skill and shrewdness Spencer Perceval, a high flying politician. Because of his slight stature and pale complexion, Perceval was given the patronising nickname "Little P" by Lord Eldon. But as a politician Perceval proved to be something of a giant.

After a legal career as a barrister and King's council, he entered Parliament as the MP for Northampton in September 1796. Once there, Perceval quickly made a name for himself as a Member with radical ideas. Although he sat on the benches of Pitt's conservative government, he was never comfortable being labelled a Tory. He always preferred to describe himself as "a friend of Mr Pitt." Indeed, many of his beliefs and ideas were far more radical than many of his fellow reformist MPs.

A devout Christian, Perceval was strongly opposed to hunting, Catholic emancipation and slavery. This last stand brought him on side with Wilberforce in his parliamentary battles to outlaw slavery. When anti-slavery was debated in the House, Perceval often crossed swords with the anti-abolitionists.

No doubt Perceval also debated with Sir William Curtis on a variety of matters ranging from shipping to the City. In fact, one of the few contemporary illustrations of Perceval speaking in Parliament shows him confronting Curtis with the speaker in the background.

But it was not just the slavery issue that set him at odds with Sir William. When the Prince of Wales instituted an inquiry into whether Caroline, his estranged wife had given birth to an illegitimate child, Perceval defended the Princess. Much to the anger of The Prince Regent and his close friends such as Curtis, Perceval's defence of Caroline was successful. In fact it was proved that she had adopted the child thus depriving the Prince of an excuse to divorce his wife.

THE CONTRACTOR AND THE CONTRACTED

In this contemporary cartoon Sir William Curtis and Spencer Perceval are squaring up to one another in front of The Speaker during a Parliamentary debate. As the title suggests, Curtis is speaking on behalf of *"The Contractors"* i.e. The City business interests and the shipping contractors of The Wapping Merchant Network. The artist has accentuated Perceval's slight appearance which earned him the nickname "Little P" from Lord Eldon.

© City of London, London Metropolitan Archives

In September 1809, Britain was ruled by a weak and divided Government. The Prime Minister, Lord Portland was in failing health and totally unable to prevent his cabinet ministers from scheming against one another.

In the case of Viscount Castlereagh, The Secretary of State for War and the Colonies and the Foreign Secretary, George Canning, this rivalry turned violent very quickly. Castlereagh, who bore responsibility for the Walcheren Expedition, became infuriated when his arch enemy Canning, interfered with the planning of the venture by ensuring Lord Chatham was given its command.

On discovering Canning's duplicity, he challenged him to a duel. On 21st September 1809, the two Ministers of The Crown faced each other with pistols drawn. Canning who had never previously handled a firearm, missed whilst Castlereagh hit him in the thigh. Even though neither man was killed, the fallout was considerable.

The ensuing scandal finally did for the frail Portland who collapsed with a stroke. Both Castlereagh and Canning were forced to resign from the Government leaving the ship of state completely rudderless.

When Perceval took over as Prime Minister on 4th October 1809, very few people thought either he or the Government would survive. But they reckoned without Perceval's courage and strength of character.

He weathered his first crisis which came in the form of an inquiry into the Walcheren Expedition. Its conclusions were highly critical of the whole enterprise and the way it was mismanaged by Lord Chatham, its commander. In view of the enquiry's damning conclusions he had little option but to resign.

Perceval foresaw how damaging this was to the Government, and banned the press from attending the proceedings. This succeeded in protecting his administration but at a high price.

The radical MP Sir Francis Burdett wrote a stinging attack on this curb of press freedom in *The Political Register* a newspaper published by William Cobbett, a fellow radical. When this landed Burdett in The Tower of London, the citizenry turned out to support him sparking bloody riots. But, the Perceval Administration survived to fight another day.

Another serious constitutional crisis followed shortly when

King George III drifted back into insanity in 1810. Perceval skilfully averted this new threat to his Government by pushing through The Regency Bill which made Prince George the effective ruler during his father's incapacity.

During all this turmoil, the Prime Minister received a strange letter from a Liverpool merchant called John Bellingham. In it, he demanded reparations from the British Government for failing to help him when he was unjustly imprisoned in Russia five years previously.

"THE WONDERFULL MAN FROM THE WEST"

It is 1810 and Sir Francis Burdett is behind bars in the Tower of London clutching a copy of the Magna Carta. On the left are the King George III, Queen Charlotte and one of the Princesses. The Prime Minister Spencer Perceval is depicted as an ass, Lord Chatham the commander of the disastrous Walcheren Expedition is a goose and Charles Yorke is a bear. Artist: James Walker.

© City of London, London Metropolitan Archives

With so many other major crises and problems to deal with, Perceval gave the letter short shrift dismissing Bellingham's claim as the ranting of an obsessive. He could not know it at the time, but this would prove to be a fatal mistake.

In the summer of 1804, John Bellingham had travelled to Russia for a short period as an export representative for British Companies in the northern port of Archangel. This was his second stint as a representative in the city, so he was no doubt picked for the job because he "knew the ropes". Such a skill was important, since doing business in nineteenth century Russia could be very tricky and sometimes dangerous for a foreigner.

By mid November of that year, he had completed his work and started his journey back to England. But, before he could leave Russia, his travel documents were seized by the authorities and he was thrown in jail. In the wrong place at the wrong time, Bellingham had become the innocent victim of a maritime legal dispute.

In the summer of the previous year, a ship called *The Soluere* had sunk in the White Sea. Although she was insured by registrars at Lloyds Coffee House in London, they informed Solomon Van Brienen, the ship's owner that they refused to pay out. Enraged, he demanded to know why the insurers were not honouring their debt. They explained that an anonymous letter had informed them the ship had been sabotaged rendering her insurance null and void.

For some reason Van Brienen suspected Bellingham of writing the letter and decided to take his revenge. Bellingham always insisted he was entirely innocent of this and he certainly had nothing to gain from writing such a missive. Perhaps he had made an enemy of Van Brienen in past dealings or perhaps the Englishman was just a convenient scapegoat. Whatever the truth, John Bellingham found himself at the receiving end of some very rough justice.

Without delay, Van Brienen went to the Military Governor of Archangel accusing Bellingham of complicity in the wreck of his ship. Needing little persuasion, the Governor seized Bellingham's travel papers and threw him in prison. Bellingham immediately appealed to Lord Granville Leveson Gower, Britain's Ambassador to the Russian Court in St Petersburg.

To be fair to Gower, he did write a letter to the Governor in Archangel requesting Bellingham's release if he was not guilty of any crime. But it seems he was really just going through motions. After receiving a reply from the Governor insisting Bellingham was justifiably imprisoned, the British diplomat dropped the matter. Numerous further requests to Gower for help from the unfortunate merchant fell on deaf ears.

For the next two years, Bellingham endured hellish Czarist prisons being beaten and fed starvation rations. Later, he would vividly sum up his ordeal in these words: *"being banded from prison to prison, and from dungeon to dungeon, fed on bread and water, treated with the utmost cruelty, and frequently marched through the streets under a military guard with felons and criminals of the most atrocious description"*

After successfully appealing to the local Procurator, Bellingham was released only to be immediately thrown back into prison. This time it was alleged that he owed a Russian merchant 2000 roubles and would be kept inside until he paid up.

For the next five years, Bellingham remained in jail whilst steadfastly refusing to pay the money. Finally, the Russian Authorities decided that this Englishman was more trouble than he was worth. He was released in 1809 and immediately deported back to England. In December of that year he finally set foot on British soil, a gaunt and dangerously embittered man. He had indeed become obsessed with the matter of gaining reparations for his unjust imprisonment.

In spite of his wife's entreaties to drop the matter, he wrote many letters to a number of people in power. These included The Foreign Secretary, Marquis Wellesley (The Duke of Wellington's brother), The Prince Regent and Spencer Perceval.

But all his efforts were in vain and by 1812, he was virtually bankrupt and in a state of total desperation. In the early part of that year, he left his wife and children at the family home in Liverpool and travelled to London. After a few more futile attempts to sway Government officials, he decided on a different course of action.

On 20th April 1812, he purchased two half-inch calibre pistols and some moulds for shot from a gunsmith called W. Beckwith at 58 Skinner Street. With their large calibre and nine inch long barrels, these were deadly weapons. He then instructed a local tailor to provide him with two nine inch deep inside pockets in a jacket he had made for him.

In the early 19th century the lobby of the House of Commons was a more public and relaxed place than it is today. Apart from a couple of officers, there was little security and the public could wander in and out of the lobby at will.

During late April and early May, Bellingham was a regular visitor to the House of Commons. As such, he became a familiar figure with both Members and officials who paid little attention to this gaunt figure dressed in black. After all, it was not unusual for visitors to be seen waiting in the lobby to petition a particular MP.

At five fifteen on the evening of 11th May, Spencer Perceval hurried into the lobby of the House of Commons. He was on his way to attend an inquiry into the Orders of State at the time, but never made it. Bellingham, who had been lurking by the entrance doors stepped forward and drawing his pistol from the coat of his jacket, fired at the Prime Minister at close range.

The musket ball smashed into Perceval's chest and tore deep into his body on a downward trajectory. According to William Smith, an MP who was in the lobby at the time, Perceval *"came towards me, looking first one way and then another, and as I thought at the moment rather like one seeking for shelter, than as the person who had received the wound, but taking two or three steps towards me, as he approached he rather reeled by me, and almost instantly fell upon the floor, with his face downwards."*

Bellingham did not attempt to flee the scene but sat down quietly on a nearby bench. He was pale and sweating, probably realising for the first time, the enormity of what had just done. Meanwhile the shot which had been heard throughout the building drew MPs and officials to the scene. One of the first of these was Sir William Curtis.

Perceval was carried to the Speaker's drawing room where he died a few minutes later whilst his assassin was taken to the bar of the house to be examined. William Curtis was one of the MPs who interrogated Bellingham. Not for the first or last time, Billy Biscuit found himself at the centre of momentous events.

No doubt the authorities were greatly relieved to discover the assassination was not the start of a revolution but a crime by a loner. In shooting Perceval, Bellingham was attacking him as a symbol of Government and not an individual.

He admitted this at his trial saying: *"I had no personal or premeditated malice towards that gentleman; the unfortunate lot had fallen upon him as the leading member of that administration which had repeatedly refused me any reparation for the unparalleled injuries I had sustained in Russia for eight years with the cognizance and sanction of the minister of the country at the court of St. Petersburg."*

But this did not lessen the magnitude of the tragedy. In firing that fatal shot, Bellingham had not only killed one of Britain's most able and honest politicians but also left his widow to care for their twelve children. The other innocent victims were John Bellingham's long suffering wife and their three children.

To add to the tragedy, Spencer Perceval had just £106 5s 1d in his bank which left his bereaved family in a state of near destitution. Fortunately, Parliament came to their aid and voted to provide £50,000 for his children and some annuities for his wife.

After a private funeral on 16th May, Spencer Perceval was interred in the Egmont vault at Charlton in South London.

On the previous day, Bellingham was put on trial for his murder, found guilty and sentenced to death. In a rare public display of emotion, the judge, Lord Chief Justice Mansfield, broke down in tears as he addressed the jury.

Bellingham was hanged on 18th May 1812, but the shock of Perceval's murder would remain with Sir William Curtis and his fellow MPs for many years to come.

CHAPTER TWENTY
1814
THE CZAR'S DINNER SERVICE

On Saturday 18th June 1814, a magnificent banquet was held in The Guildhall for Alexander I the Czar of all the Russias and The King of Prussia. It was the high point of a triumphant visit the two rulers made to England to mark their part in the defeat of Napoleon.

Sir William Curtis also attended along with the cream of London society. Under a mass of glittering chandeliers the Czar and the hundreds of other guests ate the sumptuous meal off gold plates. It was quite clear that both the Prince Regent and the British Government wanted to impress these important guests, particularly Czar Alexander.

But relations between Britain and Russia had not always been so cordial during Alexander's reign. Indeed it was only seven years since the young Czar had been in a close alliance with Britain's chief enemy, Napoleon Bonaparte of France. However, Napoleon's invasion of Russia in 1812 killed off the entente between the two nations for good. Now these recent difficulties were forgotten and political relations between the two nations were all sweetness and light.

After Russia's victories over Napoleon at the Battles of Dresden and Leipzig in 1813, Alexander arrived triumphantly at the head of his forces in Paris. From there, he and the Emperor of Prussia made their joint state visit to London.

Alexander Ist of Russia was probably the most enigmatic of all the Czars whose reign began and ended in mystery. He was brought up by his grandmother, Catherine the Great and became Czar in 1801 when his unfortunate father, Emperor Pyotr 1st was brutally murdered.

The dark circumstances surrounding this assassination by a group of drunk aristocrats and army officers were particularly murky. Since Alexander was in the Palace at the time, there was a lingering suspicion that he may at least have had knowledge of the plot.

As Czar he ruled with a strange mixture of enlightened reform

The Guildhall banquet in honour of Czar Alexander Ist and the King of Prussia on Saturday 18th June 1814. Sir William Curtis can be seen centre foreground conversing with other guests. Whilst Lady Curtis would have been with the other wives and female guests in the balconies above, the men and women of the Royal Party sit together at the table of honour at the far end of the Hall.

Sadly this highly detailed and beautiful painting by Luke Clennell carries a tragic story with it. The work was commissioned by The Earl of Bridgewater (also known as the Canals Earl because of his role in the development of Britain's inland waterways). One look at the painting shows how many VIPs Clennell had to paint to give an accurate record of the event. Unfortunately, he experienced so much difficulty in pinning down all these important personages to sit for their portraits that he suffered a mental breakdown.

After spending time in an asylum, Clennell was well enough to return home. But he did not resume work on The Guildhall Banquet painting until 1817. Once again this sparked a period of mental illness. On one occasion, members of his family discovered him hurling his brushes and paints at the canvass *"to get the proper expression"*. Somehow, he managed to complete the work but at a very high cost. This would be his last work and he never painted again until his death in 1840.

Picture © Guildhall Art Gallery, City of London

and autocracy.

Initially, his reign began well with reforms allowing freedom of the press, banning torture and drastically curtailing the activities of the secret police. There were even signs that he would finally remove the biggest stain on Russian society by emancipating the serfs. But few if any of these laws were actually enacted and by the time he came to England in 1814 he was showing increasingly autocratic tendencies.

Publicly, there was no hint of this during his visit to England. A gushing report in *The Times* on 8th June 1814 described the two monarchs as *"These two great sovereigns, to whom Europe is so deeply indebted for their glorious share in the overthrow of the general disturber of the civilised world."*

The report went on to paint a vivid picture of the landing ceremony at Dover:

"The guns of the Impregnable and the other ships of war fired a salute at the moment when the Sovereigns left the ship .... which was answered by a full discharge of artillery from the batteries on shore, and by the joyful testimonials of thousands of British people whose acclamations rent the air. The coup d'oeuil of the spectacle was magnificent; the sailors who were all dressed in new blue jackets,and white trousers, manned the yards of the vessels and joined in the plaudits of the multitudes on shore, by their honest and hearty cheerings."

This must have been a relief to Alexander who had privately harboured doubts about how he would be received in England. After all, it was only recently that he had been in an alliance with Britain's biggest enemy. In fact, he had been so concerned that he quietly sent his sister The Duchess of Oldenburg to England a week before the visit to 'test the water'.

With a hectic round of engagements and ceremonial dinners including a visit to the theatre at Oxford and a naval revue at Spithead, the State visit was an outstanding success. As the *Times* put it: *"The august party were everywhere greeted on both going and returning, with the cheers and acclamations of the people."*

It was during that sumptuous banquet at The Guildhall that Alexander was presented with a truly magnificent gift from his guests. This was a china dinner set made by Davenports, one of the finest British porcelain manufacturers. Each piece of the dinner service bore the crest of the Russian Royal House - the twin headed eagle.

After the state visit had passed and Their Majesties returned to their respective palaces, the problem of how the Davenport dinner service was to be shipped to St Petersburg had to be addressed. Sending it by one of the many merchantmen that plied the North Sea to the Baltic ports was clearly out of the question. How much of the valuable dinner service would survive a journey in one of these rough and ready vessels was anybody's guess.

No, this was a delivery that required a delicate personal and diplomatic touch and nobody was better suited to this than Billy Biscuit. He would certainly have welcomed this chance of visiting the Czar but not simply for the undoubted prestige it brought him.

At this time much of the stores for the Royal Navy were being supplied by the Baltic states. Forever the shrewd businessman, Curtis would have wanted to sound out further opportunities arising from this trade.

Also, as a founder member of the Royal Institution of Great Britain, the trip would have afforded the chance for him to further the Institution's scientific activities and links with Russia. Founded in 1799, The Royal Institution is a charity dedicated to the advancement of science and scientific knowledge. Amongst its many prominent early members were Michael Faraday, the celebrated English chemist and physicist.

Accordingly, in the mid summer of 1815, Curtis' large yacht *Die Jonge Vrow Rebecca Maria* could be seen sailing into the Gulf of Finland on the final leg of her voyage to St Petersburg. Mercifully, the weather had been fine throughout the voyage leaving the precious cargo of the Czar's Dinner Service intact.

As one of the early pioneers of seagoing yachting Curtis opted to use the *Rebecca Maria* for this particular trip with good reason. The journey to Russia would mean travelling over five hundred miles of the hostile waters of The North Sea. Curtis knew that even in the benign spring and midsummer weather, vicious storms could suddenly brew up in this grey expanse of water. Weighing 450 tons, this converted arab dhow, would be much better at dealing with foul weather than Curtis' smaller yacht *Emma*.

Czar Alexander Ist as depicted in a portrait now in
the collection of The Taganrog
Museum of Art, Rostov Oblast, Russian Federation

Undoubtedly, the hospitality that Billy Biscuit received from Czar Alexander was magnificent. He would also have been fascinated by the remarkable Russian city originally carved out of swampland by Peter The Great.

But there are no written records of the actual visit and Curtis kept no diary. Nor has it been possible to find out what happened to the dinner service. It may have survived to be on display somewhere, perhaps The Hermitage or maybe it was destroyed in The Revolution or The Second World War.

This was not the only visit that William Curtis paid to St Petersburg. In 1825, Billy Biscuit visited Russia's *"Venice of The North"* once more. On that occasion he was a passenger on Sir Willoughby de Broke's ship *HMS Antelope.*

This voyage was undertaken in the spring or summer of that year. Its purpose was probably a diplomatic goodwill visit to Alexander Ist. The presence of an Antarctic explorer, Lt Frederick Harding might also indicate that the visit also had a Royal Institution dimension. If this were the case, Sir William Curtis was included probably because of his successful "dinner service" mission ten years previously.

If the *Antelope* party actually met the Czar, then they were probably some of the last foreign visitors to see him alive. In the following autumn Alexander and his family travelled to the far south of Russia. The trip was intended to improve his wife's poor health. But ironically, it was Alexander who died first.

Allegedly, he was killed by typhus fever in the city of Taganrog in the Crimea on 19th November 1825. The Empress only survived him for a few months before dying as she accompanied her husband's remains back to his funeral in St Petersburg.

The sudden and unusual nature of Alexander's death fuelled many rumours that it was all a put up job. The most popular albeit wilder theory doing the rounds was that Alexander had secretly abdicated to become a monk. But nobody really knows the truth.

In 1925, in an attempt to put an end to all this speculation, the Soviet authorities opened the tomb in St Petersburg only to find it empty. So, like many other members of Russian Royalty, Alexander's life ended in a shroud of tragedy and mystery.

Statue of Czar Alexander Ist in modern day Taganrog.
Photo courtesy of Alexander Mirgorodskiy
Taganrog Local Government

A View of the Imperial Palace, Taganrog, Southern Russia, where Czar Alexander Ist died in 1825.
Courtesy Taganrog Local Government
www.taganrogcity.com

No pictures of Sir William Curtis' converted dhow *Die Jong Vrow Rebecca Maria* exist but this photograph of a traditional dhow taken in Qatar gives a good idea of the style of the vessel which he used for long sea journeys such as his first trip to St Petersburg in 1815.

Photograph © Rod Mattock 2010

CHAPTER TWENTY ONE
1816
THE HONOURABLE ARTILLERY COMPANY AND THE SIDMOUTH AFFAIR

The Honourable Artillery Company that William Curtis joined in about 1785 had a very ancient lineage. It still holds the proud record of being the oldest organised military unit in The United Kingdom. The HAC traditionally dates its origin from the charter to the Fraternity or Guild of Longbows, Crossbows and Handguns' which was a Guild of St George, during the reign of Henry VIII in 1537.

Before this the protection of the city's merchants and their property from the many robbers who infested the capital was done on a very ad hoc basis by vigilante groups. In 1363 a Proclamation by The Lord Mayor of London commanded those men of The City *"being strong in body"* had to *"use the recreation of bows, pellets or bolts to increase the protection of the City."*

Effectively, this was a licence for mob rule and many felons must have faced summary justice when tracked down and caught by these groups. As is the way of mob rule a number of innocent men must also have found themselves on the wrong end of a noose.

Some semblance of proper law and order only came into existence with the formation of 'trained bands' in 1573 and then not in the City until 1585. From 1611 onwards these "trained bands" became the HAC we know it today. This was when a number of members of the Company also became captains and other officers in the London trained bands

The English Civil Wars of the 17th Century saw a general fracturing of society with tragic results. Often members of the same family faced each other in battle. Royalist brother fought Parliamentarian brother and sons killed their fathers in the name of King or Parliament.

The HAC was not immune from this fratricidal conflict as its members went to war for the opposing sides. For a time, it seemed doubtful whether the Company could survive as The Civil War caused the suspension of the elections of new recruits.

During the uneasy period of Cromwellian Rule following the execution of Charles 1st, the HAC reformed. But with virtually all of its members opposed to the execution of Charles Ist this was a time of great tension between the Government and the Company. As time went on the Royalist leanings of The HAC members increased rather than lessened.

It is no doubt a tribute to the tight discipline imposed by The Captain General and his officers during this period that this did not boil over into actual confrontation with Cromwell's New Model Army. Had this happened, it is unlikely there would have been an Honourable Artillery Company for William Curtis to join a century later.

In 1658 Cromwell died marking the beginning of the end of his Brave New Puritan World. Following a two year political hiatus, the late King's son returned in 1660 and was crowned King Charles II the following year thus completing the Restoration of The Monarchy. There must have been many people throughout England who, having supported Cromwell and the Parliamentarians now genuinely feared for their safety.

The return of Royalty also marked a *"changing of the guard"* in the leadership of the HAC. King Charles II's brother, The Duke of York became Commander-in-Chief making the Regiment much more of an "establishment" organisation. Whilst this meant that ceremonial parades became much more the order of the day, the troops were still called on in times of emergency. For example, during the Gordon Riots of 1780, they were mobilised to ensure the safety of life and property in the City.

Following these disturbances, The Guildhall Court of Common Council recognised the Regiment's role in restoring the peace by passing a vote of thanks *"to the Gentlemen of The Honourable Artillery Company for their readiness to suppress the late tumultuous assemblies."* Furthermore, they stated that the tranquillity then prevailing was due principally to their loyal and prompt action.

The Company was never part of the Regular Army, but has always been a volunteer part-time regiment. Since 1908 it has been part of the Territorial Army. It differed from other regiments in another important respect. An applicant could not simply join it but their admission had to be voted on by all its existing members. Unless a prospective member was a Protestant who was well disposed towards the King they stood no chance.

By putting himself forward for election to the 450 man Regiment Billy Biscuit was concerned with more than just protecting City property. For within its ranks there were a significant number of city merchants many with overseas connections. The £3-15s joining fee was no mean sum in those days, but a price well worth paying for access to these contacts. He was accepted into The Regiment as a pikeman, the lowest rank that a gentleman could occupy.

Ostensibly, The Honourable Artillery Company is the City's own regiment of part time soldiers. In truth, they were much more a club where gentlemen dressed up to play soldiers in elaborate uniforms of white drill jackets and waistcoats with blue facings. Weekend exercises would often be enjoyable jaunts to one of London's spacious parks where the 'soldiers' would enjoy champagne picnics.

By 1803, Billy Biscuit had risen through the ranks to become Colonel of the HAC. He had done well since this was one rank below the highest office and carried many weighty responsibilities. Probably to mark this elevation in rank he presented two magnificent cannon to the HAC. They are now on display in cases at Armoury House with a plaque commemorating their distinguished donor.

In 1804, his son William followed in his father's footsteps and was admitted into the Company. As Lt Colonel Curtis he would be given an important role in a great national event two years later. On 6th January 1806 he commanded an HAC escort of the Duke of Gloucester's party at the funeral of Admiral Lord Nelson, a freeman of The Drapers Company and posthumous hero of Trafalgar.

For young William Curtis, this important role on such an historic occasion was a great honour for him and the Regiment. But it also meant a very long day for all involved starting with a parade at half past six in the morning and not ending until seven that evening. Seeing his son discharging such an important task on that day must have made Sir William Curtis very

HAC Infantry uniform of 1803    Artillery Division Uniform of 1804

Inspection of the HAC on 22 September 1803
Pictures Courtesy of The Honourable Artillery Company

proud.

Curtis senior held the post of Colonel in Chief of The Honourable Artillery Company for a further ten years. But in 1816 it came to a sudden end largely due to his own actions. As is often the case, when somebody remains in a position for a very long time they often become out of touch and arrogant. Being a fallible human being, Billy Biscuit was not immune from these failings. His nemesis would prove to be an old political acquaintance in the form of Viscount Sidmouth.

The long years of the Napoleonic Wars had left Britain in an economically weak state. This impacted particularly on the poor and the working classes in an awful cocktail of unemployment, high food prices and business failures. From 1811 a number of disturbances erupted around the country. In that year Luddites attacked mill machinery blaming mechanisation for increased unemployment.

The Home Secretary at this time was Henry Addington, Viscount Sidmouth, an unimaginative and intolerant man of limited talent. He refused to see that the many economic and social problems were the responsibility of the Government. Furthermore, he regarded the labour unrest as the work of malcontents who should be harshly suppressed.

In 1812, he refused pleas for leniency in the case of 17 Luddites who had been tried and convicted of destroying mill machinery. They were subsequently hanged in York. But far from quelling the unrest this made matters worse.

In November and December of that year Arthur Thistlewood and a group of anarchists known as Spenceans organised a series of mass meetings at Spa Fields in Islington. During the first meeting on 15th November, he called on the crowd of 20,000 to rise up and take over the Government, seize the Bank of England and occupy The Tower of London. In spite of Thistlewood's inflammatory rhetoric, the majority of the protesters remained peaceful.

On this occasion, some of the crowd then marched through Westminster complaining loudly about high food prices. Among them were a large number of distressed discharged marines and soldiers who spoke of petitioning Parliament for special welfare payments. Fortunately, troops from The Honourable Artillery Company maintained order and the demonstration passed off peacefully.

Then, one Sunday evening, the Lord Mayor was sent a copy of a letter from Lord Sidmouth stating that there were rumours that a mob intended to seize arms and armaments from The Honourable Artillery Company. He passed this information on to Colonel Curtis who put the Regiment on full alert. For two days the HAC remained under arms patrolling the streets but no disturbances occurred.

In spite of the fact that the Company's soldiers had acquitted themselves well on this occasion, the intemperate Sidmouth was not satisfied. Shortly afterwards, he summoned Colonel Curtis to an interview. In what turned out to be a severe dressing down, Sidmouth made it quite clear that he did not trust the HAC *"amateur soldiers"* to safeguard the arms and armaments held at the Regimental headquarters of Armoury House.

Riled by Sidmouth's tone and the unfair slur against the HAC, Colonel Curtis bit back in no uncertain fashion. At the end of this nasty exchange, the Home Secretary insisted that the HAC would be relieved of their arms. He would, he said, instruct The Coldstream Guards to remove all the Company's arms and ammunition to the safekeeping at The Tower of London where they were currently on duty.

The HAC Court were so scandalised by Sidmouth's comments that they resolved no military persons whatsoever, apart from their own members be admitted to Armoury House. The following day a Corporal and six men arrived from the Tower with a wagon to collect the ordinance. But their way was barred by HAC troops who sent them away empty handed.

Sidmouth was furious at this action, but short of storming Artillery House there was little he could do. The HAC had won the day and kept their weapons.

On 2nd December, there was another mass meeting at Spa Fields. This time, a group of protestors led by Doctor James Watson, one of Thistlewood's fellow anarchists looted a gun shop and marched on the Tower.

Once there they were confronted by troops who dispersed and arrested them in short order. Thanks to the cool headedness of the soldiers and their commanding officer, a bloody and tragic incident was averted.

It was this one spontaneous incident that gave the whole affair the erroneous name of The Spa Fields Riots. Thistlewood, Watson and three other conspirators were put on trial for treason which soon collapsed and the men were released. Meanwhile Billy Biscuit was facing a different trial of his own.

At the HAC Court on 18th December, Colonel Curtis was heavily criticised for single handedly carrying on such delicate negotiations with Sidmouth without referring to the Court. A resolution was passed that in future, senior officers were to refer any such matters immediately to The Court. Furthermore, no *"so called instructions"* were to be considered without the prior approval of the HAC Court and The Lord Mayor.

The Court also expressed the opinion that it would be extremely prejudicial to the discipline of The HAC for there to be such a removal of arms. The Court ordered a Guard manned by regular members to enforce this decision as of immediate effect.

Sidmouth's reaction to the Court's decision was quite out of character and strangely conciliatory. He wrote to say how happy he was that the HAC had taken such firm steps that regular troops would no longer be necessary to protect the Company's arms. This action was probably an attempt to disguise the fact that in demanding the Regiment's arms he had overstepped the mark.

This whole affair had severely wounded Curtis' pride and what he regarded as an unjust verdict still rankled. In January 1817, he wrote to the Court saying he had acted throughout solely for the good of The HAC and well being of The City of London. He added that the adverse personal comments about him made by the Court and its members gave him *"a very unpleasant feeling"*. As a result, he felt that the way this affair had been handled left him no alternative but to resign immediately.

The Court expressed its regret but said that he should not have considered surrendering the Company's ordinance to a Government Guard since this brought the HAC into contempt by both members and the wider public. The Court added that it wished to express its highest regard for Colonel Curtis' *"great exertions In his military capacity and his constant zeal in promoting the efficiency of the Company."*

Lord Sidmouth wrote to the Court saying he took *"great satisfaction in telling The Prince Regent of the Company's efficiency and loyal dedication."*

As Captain General of the HAC, The Prince Regent suggested that the Court offered the now vacant post of General to the King's brother HRH The Duke of Sussex. A written request from the Court for an audience with the Duke was swiftly acknowledged and the HAC Committee attended Kensington Palace for an official introduction to him.

However, as the Committee had received no reply from The Prince Regent to their earlier letter, they were painfully aware that their audience at The Palace might unwittingly cause offence or create future difficulties. The Duke of Sussex resolved this problem by agreeing to become a member of the HAC first and accept the post of Colonel at a later date.

All involved were well aware that having the King's brother take up the position of Colonel would mollify Curtis and remove much of the bitterness of the *"Sidmouth Affair".*

Today, the Honourable Artillery Company is part of the Territorial Army providing its only Surveillance and Target Acquisition Regiment. Members of The Regiment saw action in The South African War in 1902 as members of the City Imperial Volunteers and other units.

During The First World War it lost 1600 of its members and in The Second World War a further 723 were killed in action. More recently, the Regiment has also seen action in both Iraq and Afghanistan.

Billy Biscuit would be deeply proud of his old Company and all the men who served in it.

CHAPTER TWENTY TWO
1817
THE AFTERMATH OF THE SIDMOUTH AFFAIR

In spite of the Sidmouth Affair, it seems that Curtis remained on friendly terms with Henry Addington (Lord Sidmouth) both inside or outside Parliament. In fact, he even left him £50 in his will when he died eleven years later. This was probably because they had always been on very cordial terms. Indeed, it was Addington who recommended Curtis for a Baronetcy in 1802.

But there were many others who were not nearly so well disposed towards Lord Sidmouth. When the revolutionary Arthur Thistlewood was arrested following the Spa Fields Riots, he had already purchased tickets for a passage to America. Since they were null and void by the time he was released, he felt that The Home Secretary owed him a refund.

In 1817, he wrote Lord Sidmouth a sharp letter demanding the money for the tickets. When Sidmouth ignored his demand Thistlewood challenged the Home Secretary to a duel. This time Henry Addington responded and had Thistlewood thrown into Horsham Jail to cool his heels for twelve months.

In the meantime Sidmouth was reacting in an increasingly dictatorial and repressive manner to any form of political dissent. Playing upon the Government's fear of imminent revolution, he introduced what were known as "*The Gag Acts*" in 1817.

Under them, *Habeas Corpus* was suspended and "seditious meetings" were prohibited. Not for the first or last time a British Government had supplanted democracy with a dictatorship in the name of national security.

Not that these measures deterred the dissenters or the press for that matter. On 28th January 1817 the Prince Regent's carriage was attacked. Then on 10th March of that year, 5000 mill operatives marched from Manchester to London to petition The Prince Regent about low pay and poor working conditions.

Because they all carried blankets it became known as *"The March of The Blanketeers"*. Most were promptly arrested and imprisoned under *The Gag Acts.,* whilst the minority who resisted were severely beaten.

Then on the night of 9th June 1817, there was the Pentrich Uprising. About three hundred men led by a firebrand called Josiah Brandreth set out from the Derbyshire village of Pentrich to start a revolution by first taking over The Butterley Ironworks, then the cities of Nottingham and Newark.

Through a network of local informers Sidmouth had known what was going on all along. Indeed, one of these, a man called William Oliver, had been infiltrated into Brandreth's gang. The group were eventually confronted, dispersed and arrested by a force of twenty soldiers at the village of Giltbrook.

At the subsequent trial for treason and insurrection most of the conspirators were sentenced to deportation or long years of imprisonment. Brandreth and two other ringleaders were hanged.

No doubt, Lord Sidmouth was praised for his decisive action in quelling the Pentrich Uprising. But why, if he knew what the Pentrich Group were up to, did he not arrest them before they set out? At the time, many suspected that it did not suit his purpose.

Moreover, William Oliver may not have just been an informer but also an agent provocateur instructed by his real master, to incite the revolutionaries to greater acts of violence. This would give the Home Secretary all the excuse he needed to crack down even harder on any malcontents who dared to challenge the State. Whatever the truth, the whole business did Sidmouth's reputation no harm at all.

Throughout this turbulent period, Lord Sidmouth's instincts were to use his power as Home Secretary to crack down as hard as possible on any dissent. In this he was strongly backed by The Prime Minister Lord Liverpool who had an equally authoritarian outlook. It never occurred to the Government to address the underlying issues causing all this unrest. Their reaction to The Peterloo Massacre typified this approach.

On 16th August 1819, a crowd of 60,000 to 80,000 people gathered in St Peter's Field Manchester to demand reform of Parliamentary reform. The meeting was peaceful and presented no threat to public order. But, taking their cue from Sidmouth, the Magistrates ordered the cavalry in to disperse the gathering and arrest its leaders.

A large group of cavalry charged with sabres drawn and in the ensuing melee 15 people were killed and over 400 injured. In a satirical comparison to The Battle of Waterloo, the outrage was called The Peterloo Massacre.

Understandably, the reaction of the general public and the newspapers to Peterloo was of anger and horror. Archibald Prentice, a radical and a future editor of *The Manchester Times*, organised a petition of protest against the Massacre. In just a few days he had collected 4,800 signatures.

But Sidmouth and Lord Liverpool, the Prime Minister, showed an arrogant disregard of this public mood. On 27th August 1819 Lord Sidmouth thanked the Manchester Magistrates on behalf of The Prince Regent for their *"preservation of the public peace"*. It was an act that seemed calculated to further inflame public opinion.

The radical Robert Wedderburn declared *"The Prince is a fool with his Wonderful letters of thanks ... What is the Prince Regent or King to us, we want no King "* he is no use to us."

In an open letter, Richard Carlile, another leading radical was equally blunt:

"Unless the Prince calls his ministers to account and relieved his people, he would surely be deposed and make them all REPUBLICANS, despite all adherence to ancient and established institutions".

According to the Dictionary of National Biography, Curtis supported the Prime Minister, Lord Liverpool and Sidmouth handling this crisis. This was particularly in the case of the suspension of *Habeus Corpus*. But at this time, Curtis' main preoccupations lay elsewhere.

There is a maxim which says that all political careers end in failure, but in the case of Billy Biscuit, it was more of a gradual decline. The first signs that the clock was finally ticking on his long political career came in 1818. For some time, both the Government and Curtis' constituents in London were voicing their unhappiness about the monopolistic hold The East India Company had on so much trade in the city.

However, as their MP of many years standing Curtis was deaf to their entreaties. He stubbornly defended 'John Company' rejecting petition after petition made by his constituents. For the first time in his political life, Curtis was becoming deeply unpopular. The fact that it was well known he had a near monopoly on the supply of sea biscuits to the East India ships merely increased this unpopularity.

His friends tried to warn him about what was happening but to no avail. He insisted on his right to back whosoever served the interests of the City best. Furthermore, he brushed off any suggestions that he was acting for vested interests saying he had always been whiter than white in all his dealings. In the election of 1818, the inevitable happened and he was ejected from his Parliamentary seat.

Characteristically, Billy Biscuit took it all in his stride. Instead of sulking he threw a lavish banquet for his old friend The Prince Regent, the Royal Dukes and members of the cabinet. Tearfully, the Prince promised to find Curtis a safe seat in the country somewhere. But he would hear none of it saying he had no wish to be under an obligation to the Prince or anyone else.

Others urged him to take up the peerage as Lord Tenterden. He was briefly tempted by this suggestion since his wife had property interests in that area of Kent. But the idea was firmly squashed by Lady Curtis who made it be known that she had no wish to be considered a mere chattel of a Lord. If Billy was his own man then his wife was also very much her own woman.

In February 1819, he became an MP representing the rotten borough of Bletchingley in Surrey, but remained in post for only about a year. Although this beautiful little village consisted of only 85 buildings and had a population of about 500 it actually returned two MPs at that time.

Elections for its members took place in the local pub called *The White Hart Inn.* There are no records explaining why Sir William's tenure as one of its MPs was so brief. Since the other Member was a Whig called Matthew Russell, it is likely this was a short term pairing arrangement between the two main parties in The House of Commons.

In 1820 Curtis was back as MP for London and remained in Parliament as *"The Father of The Commons"* for another six years. But in 1826, he again tasted the bitterness of defeat and unpopularity when defending his City seat during the General Election. On this occasion, he abandoned his campaign before polling day. If the poster shown on the next page is anything to go by, he may have realised for the first time in his life how unpopular he had become. It must have been a severe shock to this sick man who only had another three years to live. This would have seemed unthinkable just ten years previously, but times were changing and Billy Biscuit's era would soon be past.

He finally became MP for Hastings in 1826, but he was now in very poor health and of advancing years. Curtis had long been plagued by gout which often prevented him from attending the Commons in London. In December of that year he bowed to the inevitable and resigned his seat. He retired to his home at Cliff House in Ramsgate with his devoted wife Anne and died in January 1829.

The curtain had finally fallen on the long and remarkable career of one of the last and greatest Georgian merchant princes.

The shine finally wears off. A virulent and sarcastic anti-Curtis election poster probably published during his aborted campaign to defend his City of London seat in 1826.

© London Metropolitan Archive

CHAPTER TWENTY THREE
1822
'ONE AND TWENTY DAFT DAYS'
GEORGE IV'S SCOTTISH VISIT

It was a cold and wet afternoon on 14th August 1822 when *The Royal George*, King George IV's elegant yacht was towed into the Firth of Forth near Edinburgh by the steam ships *James Watt* and *Comet*.

Accompanying the King at his request on his first official visit to Scotland was his close friend, Sir William Curtis. Billy Biscuit was delighted by this great honour and willingly sailed to Scotland in his own expensive and substantial yacht *Die Jong Vrou Rebecca Maria*.

As torrential rain battered the yachts, a barge pulled up alongside *The Royal George*. On board was the distinguished author Sir Walter Scott, the mastermind and organiser of the Royal Visit. Scott was anything but happy that afternoon. Not only had he just received news of the death of his close friend William Erskine, he had to inform the King that, due to the bad weather, the official landing should be postponed until the following morning. It was not an auspicious start for the first visit by a reigning British monarch to Scotland since 1650.

The King's erratic fits of anger were common knowledge, so Scott had no idea how his Sovereign would greet such news. The very painful rash that was currently afflicting him further darkened his mood. As the barge nudged up against the Royal Yacht his emotions were in a turmoil.

But Scott need not have worried. On hearing of his arrival, King George rushed to the rail and exclaimed with delight:

"What! Sir Walter Scott! The man in Scotland I most want to see! Let him come up."

After a welcoming speech by Sir Walter, the King toasted him with Cherry brandy, his favourite tipple. Scott hid his glass in his pocket to keep as a Royal souvenir. At three that afternoon, the Royal Party sat down to dinner with Scott on the King's right and Sir William Curtis on his left.

Fortunately, the foul weather did not last and the King was

able to disembark in brilliant sunshine the following day. Dressed in full Naval uniform, he stepped onto a red carpet littered with flowers and lined by cheering crowds.

At last as organiser of the Royal Visit, Scott could breathe a sigh of relief. Although eventually a big success, the Royal Visit was punctuated by unintentionally comic incidents.

The first of these occurred even before George arrived in Scotland. A pageant to mark the King's birthday on Monday 12th August saw a colourful procession of carriages escorted by a ceremonial guard of Highlanders and members of the Midlothian Yeomanry make its way from Edinburgh Castle to Holyroodhouse. On board the carriages were dignitaries carrying The Regalia of Scotland.

But before this cavalcade could travel very far, it was halted by a horseman dressed in the full garb of a highland warrior. This was the flamboyant and fiery Alasdair Ranaldson MacDonell of Glengarry, the head of The Society of True Highlanders. As the cream of Edinburgh Society waited, with a mixture of impatience and embarrassment, Glengarry demanded what he saw as his right as a Highland Chieftain to lead the procession.

Fortunately, after a few well chosen and diplomatic words by Captain Ewan MacDougall, Glengarry thought better of his demand and rode off. Without further ado, the procession continued its stately journey to Holyrood. History does not record whether the good Captain was promoted for saving the day, but he certainly deserved to be.

George's official visit to Scotland was first suggested shortly after his Coronation in the previous year. The visit had a serious intent since the King was very unpopular with the general public because of the perceived mistreatment of his estranged wife Caroline of Brunswick. Added to this was the fear that the virus of revolution so recently engulfing France and America could spread to Britain and tear the Union between Scotland and England apart.

Only two years before, there had been serious and violent unrest in Scotland. Following the end of the Napoleonic Wars, Britain was plunged into an economic recession. This was exacerbated by the many underlying grievances about poor pay and conditions felt by the working classes.

Nowhere was this hardship felt more keenly than in central Scotland around the cities of Glasgow and Edinburgh. On Saturday April 1st 1820, 60,000 workers had gone on strike in Glasgow demanding not only better working conditions but an overall reform of Government.

The state's fears of revolution and insurrection were further strengthened on Monday 3rd April 1820 when a group of radicals marched on the ironworks at Carron to seize weapons. On a sloping area of farmland called Bonnymuir, near Falkirk, the Radicals numbering not more than fifty confronted a mixed group of local and militia and Hussars. Taking cover behind a stone wall they shot at the troops who returned fire. The cavalry then charged up the slope and through a gap in the wall. The radicals were quickly scattered by the Hussars who killed some and took nineteen others prisoner.

In a subsequent trial, one of the ring leaders John Wilson, was found guilty of *"compassing to levy war against the King in order to compel him to change his measures"*.Despite a plea for leniency, he was hanged and posthumously decapitated in front of a crowd of 20,000 people.

Two other of the leaders of what would become known as *The Radical War* were also tried and sentenced to death. Once again the authorities were deaf to all pleas for mercy and Andrew Hardie and John Baird were also publicly hanged and beheaded in Stirling. This time the crowd was much smaller, estimated at no more than 2000.

Whether or not this was because of intimidation by the authorities or general 'violence fatigue' is difficult to say, but the *Radical War* had given the authorities a bad fright. What was needed was a bit of pageantry to distract the populace and who better to provide it than King George IV?

But the government of Lord Liverpool in London also had another hidden agenda for the Royal visit. They had recently received the bills for the King's visit to Ireland and were shocked at the cost of the Monarch's lavish entertaining. The leaders of the major imperial European powers including George were due to attend the signing of The Treaty of Verona. Afraid that a further round of expensive Royal entertaining would empty the Exchequer, the Government seized upon the *Scottish Jaunt* as a more cost effective alternative.

There was also a further sexual and political dimension to all this. On his recent visit to Ireland, George had become greatly enamoured with Lady Elizabeth Conyngham, the wife of the Anglo-Irish owner of Slane Castle. Indeed, the couple had become so attached that the King refused to travel anywhere without his new mistress.

The problem was that Lady Conyngham was at daggers drawn with the wife of the Foreign Secretary Lord Castlereagh. The animosity between the two ladies was so great it would have been impossible for them to travel in the same party to Verona.

It would also have been unthinkable for the King to travel without his Foreign Secretary to such an important event. Since Lord Castlereagh would not attend without his wife, it was agreed that he would represent the King at The Congress of Verona whilst the Monarch visited Scotland.

Although this was greeted with huge sighs of relief from the British Government, others were not so happy. Prince Metternich, the Macchiavellian spymaster of the Austro-Hungarian Empire had longed for the opportunity to manipulate the malleable George once he was in Verona. But a British delegation led by the spiky Castlereagh was an entirely different ball game. How European politics might have been shaped had George gone to Verona is one of history's many fascinating ifs.

As it was, the Royal visit to Scotland was considered no mere sideshow, but an important event in itself. No British monarch had visited Scotland since 1650 and there was a great deal of ill feeling between the two nations to be assuaged.

It seems that Sir Walter Scott was the personal choice of George to organise such a visit. A great romanticist, especially where Scottish history was concerned, Scott set about his allotted task with great relish. What he achieved was little short of the reinvention of the Highland Tradition that persists to this day.

For the great writer, this was the golden opportunity to bring his romanticised image of Scotland and his vision of the heroic Highlanders to life. Scott wanted the King's visit to be a *Tartan Pageant* which would bring *Waverley*, his romantic novel of the Highlands, into reality. As far back as 1815, George had already been persuaded by Scott that he was the *New Jacobite King of Scotland*. As such, the Monarch would be the centrepiece of this

King George IV's yacht *The Royal George* arrives in Leith Harbour
at the start of The Royal Visit to Scotland in 1822.
Painting by Thomas Buttersworth

The Royal procession into Edinburgh at the start of King George's visit to
Scotland in 1822 by John Wilson Ewbank
Pictures Courtesy City Art Centre Edinburgh

elaborate pageant.

But there was a serious problem. Following the crushing of the Jacobite Rebellion in 1745, the wearing of tartan by the Highland Clans had been banned under The Dress Act. Although this was repealed in 1782, the general wearing of tartans by ordinary Highland people had fallen into disuse.

By the 1820s, tartans were only regularly worn by troops in the British Army. So it was to this source that Scott turned when searching for enough tartan material for his *plaided pageant*. He also approached the traditional Highland Chiefs or Lairds for their help in realising his vision.

He probably wished he had not since they spent much of their time squabbling. The prickly Alasdair Ranaldson MacDonell of Glengarry soon took umbrage because his Society of True Highlanders were not given pride of place in the proceedings. For a time, this combination of infighting and serious questions about King George's health placed The Royal Visit in the balance.

Fortunately Scott was able to ignore Glengarry's objections and press on with the organisation of the visit. But MacDonnell was not content to leave matters there as his upstaging of the King's birthday celebrations showed. By the summer George's health had also sufficiently improved and in August, the stage was set for what would become known as *"The King's Scottish Jaunt."*

Before, the Royal Visit could proceed however, there was the important question of the Royal attire. Once again, Sir Walter Scott came to the fore, persuading the King that he should dress himself in *The Garb of old Gaul*. In practice this meant dressing George in a tasteless caricature of a Highlander.

No detail was spared by the tailors in creating this Royal tartan outfit. It dripped with jewelled saltires, eagle feathers and a crown of Scotland made of diamonds, pearls, rubies and emeralds. In addition to a jewelled dirk and belts of finest Morroccan leather no less than 61 yards of satin, 31 yards of velvet and 17½ yards of cashmere were used to create the outfit.

The total price came to the staggering sum of £1,354. 18s. But apart from the huge cost, the whole outfit must have been unbearably hot for the obese and unfit King to wear.

Presumably wishing to emulate his Royal friend, Sir William Curtis had a similarly elaborate and rather tasteless tartan outfit made up for the visit. But this would prove to be his only major gaffe of the whole tour.

This occurred at a Levee held at Holyroodhouse on Saturday 17th August. On this occasion the cream of Edinburgh and Scots society queued up to be formally introduced to George. Few members of that gathering were prepared for the sight that greeted them.

Dressed in his tailor made tartan outfit, the King was also wearing pink pantaloons to conceal his bloated legs. Whilst some were offended by the shortness of the King's tartan, Lady Hamilton-Dalrymple made light of this saying:

"Since he is to be among us for so short a time, the more we see of him the better."

The sight of Sir William Curtis also dressed in full Highland fig seemed to have caused many present equal offence. Whether this extended to the King or whether George was just mildly amused at his friend is open to question.

But without doubt, the Monarch and his old friend's dubious dress sense opened them both to merciless public ridicule. In the following weeks cartoonists such as Cruikshank and Gilray had a field day satirising both men with cruel caricatures.

For Billy Biscuit, who had uncomplainingly born the brunt of the cartoonists' satire for many years, this was the last straw. Their lampooning of him during his Scottish foray left a bitter taste that lasted for the rest of his life.

But heedless of the London satirists' poison arrows, the Royal Tour continued apace. On one occasion, George entertained no less than 457 ladies in the King's Room. As etiquette demanded he had to kiss each one of the bejewelled ladies with their ostrich feathers, on the cheek. This was no hardship for the Monarch whatsoever.

Generally, George IV's visit to Scotland was judged to be a great success. Perhaps the highlight of the whole tour occurred on Thursday 22nd August 1822 when the King waved to a wildly enthusiastic crowd from the battlements of Edinburgh Castle.

Despite the heavy rain, a densely packed crowd of many

Cruikshank cartoon showing King George IV admonishing Sir William Curtis for bringing ridicule on them both for wearing a similar tartan outfit at The Holyroodhouse Levee. Picture Courtesy City Art Centre Edinburgh

King George IV kissing the 457 ladies in The King's Room. Sir William Curtis who is in the centre of the picture is saying: *"My God! But this is warm work. It is lucky we are so thinly clad."*
Picture Courtesy City Art Centre Edinburgh

thousands returned the King's waves with huge cheers. George, who had become used to much less enthusiastic receptions South of the Border was clearly moved:

"*Good God! What a fine sight!*" He exclaimed. "*I had no conception there was such a fine scene in the world; and to find it in my own dominions; and the people are as beautiful and as extraordinary as the scene.*"

He even made light of the exceedingly damp weather saying:

"*Rain? I feel no rain. Never mind, I must cheer the people.*"

The Royal visit finally ended on the following Thursday having achieved all that Sir Walter Scott had hoped. The Government and the King's advisers also breathed a big sigh of relief as the steam ships *The Comet* and *The James Watt* towed *The Royal George* out of the Firth of Forth for the long return journey south.

One of many innuendo laden cartoons poking fun at King George IV
Courtesy City Art Centre, Edinburgh

CHAPTER TWENTY FOUR
BILLY BISCUIT AND THE SPANISH REFUGEES
GIBRALTAR 1823

Whilst George IV and Sir William Curtis were being lavishly feted during the King's visit to Scotland, the final act of a long running tragedy was unfolding in Continental Europe. Although he did not know it yet, Sir William Curtis was to play a role at the very end of this drama.

In August 1822, The Congress of Verona was convened in that beautiful and ancient Italian city. Its main purpose was for the Imperial Nations of Austria, Russia, Prussia, England and France to carve Europe up into their respective spheres of influence. This would be the completion of a process that had begun with the Congress of Vienna in 1815.

But the beginning of this glittering occasion was overshadowed by two dark events. The first was the tragic suicide of Lord Castlereagh, the head of the British delegation. Occurring on the eve of the Conference, his place was hurriedly taken by the Duke of Wellington. The second event was the continued imprisonment of King Ferdinand VII of Spain by the revolutionary Government that had seized control of the country two years previously.

In 1813, Ferdinand VII had been restored to the Spanish throne following the end of Napoleonic occupation. But, the delight of the local population to see the back of the French oppressor was short lived. It soon became apparent that they had swapped a foreign tyrant for a home grown one. For instead of taking this golden chance to go down in history as an enlightened ruler, Ferdinand became a cruel and capricious autocrat.

Inevitably this led to increasing unrest and opposition to his rule. In 1820, the Spanish Army under Colonel Rafael Riego revolted, overthrowing Ferdinand and taking him prisoner. He would remain the revolutionaries' hostage for a further three years.

Ironically, this did not suit the French Government even though they had executed their own Monarchy a mere 30 years earlier. Now, instead of applauding revolutionaries in neighbouring Spain, they feared them. It would be all too easy for the unrest to spill over the frontier plunging France into a second Great Terror. Something had to be done.

At the Congress, the majority of the other Nations also expressed alarm at the revolutionary turmoil occurring in Spain. Taking advantage of this, the French Government pressed for their support for an armed intervention in Spain to restore Ferdinand VII to the throne. The Austrians, Russians and Prussians agreed to back the French intervention. But Britain's role in all this was, at best, ambivalent. Whilst frowning on any intervention, she stood firmly on the sidelines.

On 23rd April 1823, a French Army of one hundred thousand troops crossed the Pyrenees to free Ferdinand and reinstate him as King of Spain. From the very start, the Spanish Revolutionaries were no match for the vastly superior French Army under the Generalship of the Duc d'Angoulême. Over the next six months, the retreating Spanish forces were steadily pushed further and further south finally making a stand at Cadiz.

For weeks, the Revolutionaries held the strategic Fort Trocadero against French attacks and bombardment. Because the fort controlled the only land access to Cadiz, the French were unable to take the city.

Then on 31st August 1823, The French Army mounted a massed attack and took the fort. This paved the way for a sustained bombardment of Cadiz itself. Finally, on 23rd September 1823, the Revolutionary Cortes (Parliament) bowed to the inevitable and surrendered to the French.

Once Ferdinand had been re-installed as King, he forgot his promises of amnesty for the rebels and unleashed a terrible campaign of reprisals. Accurate figures are hard to come by but in the following years, thousands of Spaniards were executed and imprisoned for supporting the rebellion. Colonel Rafael Riego, the leader of the revolt was hanged in Madrid on 7th November 1823.

In the autumn and winter of 1823 hundreds of traumatised and starving Spanish refugees crossed the border into Gibraltar. By early December this influx was straining the resources of the tiny British Colony. Without enough food to go around, starvation and disease

These cannon would have been guarding the Rock when Billy Biscuit visited in 1823
Photo courtesy Government of Gibraltar

Trafalgar Cemetery, Gibraltar where many of the British sailors killed in The Battle of Trafalgar are laid to rest.
Picture courtesy Government of Gibraltar

threatened. There must also have been a fear that the presence of so many republican refugees could provide a pretext for the Spanish to invade Gibraltar.

As luck would have it, Sir William Curtis was sailing to Naples in his converted dhow, *The Rebecca Maria* at the time. In early December, his yacht and its naval escort, the brig *HMS Weasel* dropped anchor in The Bay of Gibraltar.

The ultimate destination of Curtis' party and the fact that he was travelling with a naval escort provides a strong indication that this was an official mission rather than a pleasure cruise. At the time, The King of Naples and Sicily was the only friend the British had in the Mediterranean. In which case an official visit as a show of support to the King would have been timely indeed.

No doubt, during his stop in Gibraltar, Curtis hoped to pay a courtesy visit to the Governor, Lord Chatham whom he had last seen on the disastrous Walcheren expedition in 1809.

But instead, he was greeted by a delegation of two worried local dignitaries. Explaining the plight of the refugees and the inability of the local administration to cope, they pleaded with Curtis for financial help. How much did they need? Curtis asked. The answer was £1000 - a breathtaking £75,000 in today's values.

In a subsequent letter to *The Times*, William Rangeston a prominent local businessman took up the story:

Considerable wagers were offered and taken, that he (Curtis) would give a check for one thousand pounds. Accordingly, two of the gentlemen deputed to wait on him by the Committee, went on board his schooner and were received by Sir William in the most gracious manner who not only made them partake of delicacies such as could not be obtained in this hemisphere but astonished them with a check upon his banking house for the very amount named by his friends, and which, thank God, has relieved the wants of hundreds who otherwise must have sunk under their sufferings"

It is clear from Rangeston's paean of praise for Sir William' Curtis' generosity that his philanthropic act had saved the lives of many of those unfortunate refugees.

In a further act of generosity Sir William offered free passage to Naples for any members of the exiled Cortes. Thus, these fugitives who must have been at the top of King Ferdinand VII's 'Most Wanted' list, were put well and truly out of harm's way.

Two views of Gibraltar showing the Rock, harbour and the Bay.
Pictures courtesy The Government of Gibraltar
www.gibraltar.gov.uk

CHAPTER TWENTY FIVE
CRIME AND PUNISHMENT
IN BILLY BISCUIT'S TIME

Contemporary newspapers give a vivid insight into criminal activity in the time of Billy Biscuit. Murders feature with monotonous regularity providing a salutary reminder that such crime has been rife since Cain and Abel. What is striking from many of the reports is not only the shockingly casual nature of such crimes, but the failure of the perpetrators to foresee the consequences of their actions.

On 16th December 1786, *The Times* reported on a trial for a crime that was all too common in the back streets of London. On this occasion a gang of pickpockets led by an unsavoury character called "Irish Mick" Walker attacked a shopkeeper called Duncan Robinson with knives. *The Times* spares their readers none of the lurid details when describing the evidence of the attending surgeon:

"His account of the wounds of the deceased were dreadful in the extreme. He had received one which, beginning at the root of the hair, passed over the hollow of the eye and nearly divided his nose. Another, on his shoulder was six inches long and more than an inch deep. And a third stroke had nearly divided the tendons of his left wrist."

After lying delirious on his bed *"in a gore of blood"* Robinson finally expired. Irish Mick and his two accomplices were sentenced to death by the judge, Baron Hotham.

It is clear from the report that one of these, a Richard Payne, who was in his early teens, had not actually struck any of the fatal blows.

However, this did not save him. Baron Hotham observed: *"that though he had not struck a blow, yet it was a maxim in law, that persons connected for a felonious purpose, if any evil consequences ensued, were all equally answerable for the guilt."*

He left it up to the jury to decide Payne's ultimate fate. *"The Jury without hesitation brought in their verdict Guilty ! Death!"*

All too many murders were perpetrated on women in a cruelly casual fashion. Undoubtedly, this reflected the low level of protection women enjoyed in Georgian society.

For example, on 13th August 1788, *The Times* reported a "*Cruel Murder!*" of a young girl called Miss Cordridge *"A beautiful young girl of seventeen years of age."*

Reflecting not only the outrage of its readers but their desire for the most ghoulish details, the report continues: *In short her murderer was her seducer by whom she was pregnant. He had appointed to meet her in a barn where the wretch nearly severed her head from her body and afterwards secreted her remains in a ditch. This inhuman wretch is only 18 years of age, of a very good family, named Hartley; and the only reason he gives for committing this foul crime is, that his family considered her inferior and objected to their union.*

In these early days of journalism no consideration was given to the effect that such partisan reporting had on a fair trial. The reasoning was simple: if a perpetrator like young Hartley was caught and confessed then any trial was considered a mere formality.

Of course murder was not the only crime that occurred in Georgian England. In one case Sir William Curtis was himself the victim of a suspected arson attack.

This happened on an area of woodland he had inherited from his late brother Timothy in Frimley Common, Surrey. On 6th May 1824 a huge blaze broke out in suspicious circumstances destroying a very large number of mature fir trees.

Sir William Curtis was furious suspecting that it was an act of revenge by local malcontents against his late brother. He determined to take the strongest legal action against those he deemed responsible. The fact that he invoked The Black Act against all the inhabitants in the Hundred of Godleyhurst where the fire took place is a measure of his anger.

The Black Act was a particularly harsh piece of legislation passed in 1723 to crack down on deer poaching in private parks, its main target was a gang of poachers known as the *Wokingham Blacks*. They were called this because they blackened their faces to avoid detection when poaching at night. The Act made it a hanging offence to be in a park with arms or stealing deer with blackened faces. No doubt the gang members revelled in the extra notoriety such a name gave them.

A common sight in the 18th Century. The public hanging of a pirate at Execution Dock, Wapping. It is said that felons bodies were covered by three tides before being cut down.

© City of London, London Metropolitan Archives

Because there was some doubt about whether or not this fire had been arson, the authorities decided this was a civil case. As such, there was never a possibility of the Death Penalty being invoked. But if the case went in Curtis' favour, the consequences for the locals would have been very hard indeed.

But although arson was strongly suspected, nothing could be proved against any individuals. The Jury duly found for the defendants to the great relief of the local community.

On occasions, Sir William Curtis also sat with the Lord Mayor to adjudicate cases in his capacity as a magistrate of London. The offences that came before them would vary widely from a case of petty forgery to more serious matters.

On 29th October 1804, a defendant called George Hart appeared before Sir William charged with forging his references to gain service as a porter. Unable to pay the fine of £20, he was jailed in The House of Correction for one month.

A much more serious offence came before Sir William in The Guildhall in April 1804. Thomas and Elizabeth Wood, a husband and wife team of criminals appeared before him charged with robbing a poor woman of her meagre belongings.

More seriously in the eyes of the law was the discovery of coin counterfeiting equipment at Wood's House. This comprised crucibles, dyes and punches to make counterfeit sixpences and shillings and aqua fortis compound to give fake coins the appearance of silver. In this case the couple were held for further examination.

No record is available of the couple's ultimate fate but it was unlikely to have been a happy one. Coin and currency forgery had long been capital offences with the death penalty regularly being invoked. As a hardened criminal with plenty of form, Thomas Woods must have known the dire situation he and his wife now found themselves in. It is indeed ironic that an act of petty theft carrying a short jail sentence had led them to being on trial for their lives.

In Georgian times, coin clipping was particularly popular amongst the cleverer and less violent members of the criminal classes. This crime was especially prevalent in the seventeenth and eighteenth centuries when coins were usually cast in pure silver or gold.

Basically, criminals would clip a sliver of metal off the side of a gold coin to store up and melt down when there was a sufficient quantity. Then it would be sold either as bullion or cast into counterfeit coins.

In the 17th century the problem of counterfeiting using clipping was so great that it threatened to destabilise the currency and the economy of England. This is probably why it was punishable by death as the Reverend Robinson of Thurstonland near Huddersfield discovered. In 1690, he was caught coin clipping and duly executed.

Despite this draconian law, coin clipping continued well into the 19th century. According to reports in *The Ipswich Journal* of 6th December 1828, a Mr Lavender of Manchester was caught with *"base coin to the amount of £1160"* which he had made in Mrs Merton's house in Leigh Street, Manchester. By today's values that would equate to over £78,000 a truly staggering sum to have been counterfeited by one man. It is unlikely that Lavender lived to spend it.

By coincidence, the same issue of *The Ipswich Journal* had reports relating to two crimes of which Billy Biscuit was indirectly the victim. The first was actually due to suspected coin clipping. One day in early December, a porter of Sir William Curtis' company took six hundred guineas to be deposited in The Bank of England. When weighing the coins, the bank's clerk discovered that 115 of them were too light and put them to one side.

The Ipswich Journal reported with perhaps a hint of admiration for the audacity of the crime that: *"Whilst the porter was arranging the notes he had received from the clerk, some thief contrived to abstract the 115 light guineas with which he got clean off, and has not yet been apprehended."*

The recovery of the stolen coins was about as likely as the careless porter hanging on to his job.

The second report relates how a prisoner named Joseph Hunton was visited in jail by the The Reverend Mr Cotton whilst awaiting execution.

"The Ordinary reports that on entering the cell of Hunton, he found him in the most deplorable state of mind and his appearance denoted the deepest despair." This in fact marked the end of one of the most celebrated forgery cases of the late

Georgian period and whose victim was Sir William Curtis' own bank.

Joseph Hunton originally started business as a draper in his native town of Great Yarmouth. By 1811, he was sufficiently successful to issue his own coinage in the form of silver shilling tokens to be exchanged for goods at his business and those of a fellow draper called Blyth in Bury St Edmunds.

By the mid 1820s it seems that Hunton felt he had outgrown his Yarmouth business and moved to London. It was from that time that the clock started counting down to Joseph Hunton's eventual destruction.

Initially, his London drapery business went extremely well for this canny businessman. After a relatively short time he had amassed a fortune worth £30,000 or nearly £2,000,000 in today's money.

If Hunton had just played safe and left it at that he may well have died in his bed, a respected city father. But like many such entrepreneurs, he became convinced of his own invulnerability. In a search to increase his wealth, he plunged into much riskier ventures. He took the unwise decision to play the stock market losing all his money speculating on Spanish bonds. Faced with imminent bankruptcy he decided that his only salvation was to forge Bills of Exchange.

Hunton was sufficiently clever and resourceful man to make crime pay for quite a time. In fact this little bespectacled man dressed in his sober Quaker hat and suit, became a well known and respected figure in The City of London. He certainly seemed to be prospering in business since he purchased a large house and estate in Capper Street, Walthamstow. Once installed there with his wife and twelve children, he spent large sums of money improving the garden and grounds.

This outwardly pious family man, excited so much admiration from everyone that nobody seems to have asked where all his money actually came from. That is until, like many master criminals, Hunton overreached himself. By 1828, he had been forging Bills of Exchange without being caught for some considerable time. Flushed with this success he flooded the market with counterfeit Bills.

This proved Hunton's undoing finally alerting the Committee

Of Bankers for the Prevention of Frauds and Forgeries. It was not long before the trail led them to the Quaker businessman. Two of the bills valued at £43. 4 shillings and £179 (approximately £2,900 and £12,000 in modern money) were issued in the name of Edward Wilkins of Abingdon whom, it turned out had died eight days before the Bills were issued. These and other fraudulent bills had been presented to Sir William Curtis' bank.

Before he could be arrested, Hunton was tipped off and went on the run with a price of £200 on his head. Much to the frustration of Forrester, the City Officer pursuing him, the trail then went cold. One of William Curtis' sons even went to Calais and Paris with Mr Cope, The City Marshall following alleged sightings of Hunton. But they proved to be a case of mistaken identity.

A few days later, dressed in his Quaker attire and carrying a passport in his own name, Hunton boarded a French steam packet bound for Boulogne which was moored by The Tower of London. Even now with his back to the wall Joseph Hunton showed extraordinary brass face in laying several false trails. *The Morning Post* of 9th October 1828 reported that:

"He however, soon afterwards left this steamer, but not without first circulating some religious tracts among passengers and crew and to some of the latter he read a lecture on the abomination of swearing."

Then, quickly changing into a light green frock, a pair of light grey pantaloons, a black stock and a foraging cap, he swapped the French ship for a nearby Leeds steam packet bound for New York. His disguise was so good, that officers who boarded the vessel searching for him, did not think for one moment, that *"Mr Wilkinson the merchant from Portsmouth"* was their man.

It is quite likely that Joseph Hunton would have escaped to the New World were it not for a chance discovery by Forrester. In a bid to stop him leaving the country, he had travelled to Plymouth following one of many clues to the fugitive's whereabouts. By this time, the authorities had worked out that Mr Wilkinson the Portsmouth merchant and Joseph Hunton were one and the same.

At the Plymouth Post Office he was told that *"a little man called Mr Wilkinson"* had been enquiring after letters from his wife in London. But as Hunton a.k.a. Wilkinson was already at sea bound for New York, it seemed he was beyond the grasp of English justice.

However, once again, fate intervened on behalf of Forrester, this time in the form of bad weather. The Leeds packet bound for New York had been delayed by stormy seas off Spithead. Braving the mountainous waves, the dogged Forrester and another officer called Hunt sailed the treacherous ten mile stretch of water to where the ship was anchored waiting for the storms to abate.

Once aboard, they went down to Hunton's cabin on the pretext of delivering an important letter to Mr Wilkinson. Hunton took the letter fully expecting it to be from his wife. Instead he opened sheet of paper which was blank except for the signature of Mr Gates, the Solicitor to the Committee of Bankers. Joseph Hunton visibly paled realising that the game was finally up.

In the cabin, the officers also found two letters. One was to the editor of *The Times* insisting that his forgeries were nowhere near as great as had been reported. Furthermore, it demanded an apology and correction stating that he would return to pay off all his debts as soon as possible.

The other was to Sir William Curtis' Bank informing them that *"as it was not convenient for the firm to discount any more bills for him, he would absent himself from London for a short time."* In an attempt to throw the authorities off the scent both letters bore an address at Deal in Kent, somewhere that Hunton had never visited during his flight from justice. For whatever the reason, they were not sent.

Hunton's trial for forgery began at the end of October 1828 at The Old Bailey amidst great public interest. *The Morning Chronicle* reported that *"The Court was crowded to excess, amongst whom were several members of The Society of Friends."*

Although he was suspected of defrauding the Curtis Bank of £5000, Hunton was standing trial for forging only three Bills amounting to a total of £264. Characteristically, he pleaded not guilty to all charges. Probably realising his client had little chance of acquittal, his brief, a Mr Phillips played a classic legal delaying tactic. He challenged no less than twenty of the men put up as jurors.

The Judge, Mr Justice Park was clearly exasperated by this

move commenting that he had never before encountered a case where 20 jurors, the maximum number allowed, had been challenged. After some delay, a fresh jury was sworn in, but Hunton had another trick up his sleeve.

Passing a note to the Judge, he requested an adjournment, claiming that having been deprived of all his books he *"had no means of defence whatsoever."* But the Justices were having no more of the defendant's delaying tactics and ordered the trial to proceed.

Finally, Hunton exhausted the patience of even his own defence counsels by repudiating them. At this point, they reportedly *"threw up their briefs"* leaving him to fend for himself. Although Hunton's chances of being found not guilty were always very slim, the loss of his defence team definitely sealed his fate. In early November 1828, he was found guilty of all charges and was sentenced to death by hanging.

This took place on 8th December 1828 in front of a large crowd assembled at Newgate Prison. There were probably many in that throng who believed the authorities would not actually hang *one of their own.* Probably like Hunton himself, they thought he would be spared by a last minute reprieve. But they were wrong and with a crash the trap opened sending the forger to his maker. He was 58 and left a widow and twelve children.

It is thought that by the time Joseph Hunton was apprehended, his forging activities had netted him between four and five million pounds by today's monetary values. Although this and his arrest after an exciting manhunt helped to add interest to his trial there was another factor that made it such an event of great interest. For it was one of the very few trials where a Quaker was tried and hanged for a Capital Offence.

In fact, his relationship with The Society of Friends had been tarnished by an unexplained incident long before he arrived in London. The details remain a mystery, but knowing Hunton it probably involved a "misunderstanding" about money.

His pious ways and sober Quaker clothes for which he was well known around the City, were simply a camouflage for his nefarious activities. Having said that, The Quakers proved their metal by sticking by him to the very end.

Two elders of The Society of Friends sat with him the whole

night before his execution. Another, a Mr Sparks Moline, accompanied him to the steps of the scaffold.

Just over a month later, Hunton's main victim, Sir William Curtis also died. His passing was in the style that the forger would no doubt have wished for himself - quietly in his bed as a respected pillar of the community.

CHAPTER TWENTY SIX
1823 TO 1829
ROYAL RAMSGATE

Following his Coronation in 1820, etiquette dictated that King George IV should visit his other dominion of Hanover. He did this 24th September 1821, but instead of leaving from Dover as was the usual Royal custom, he chose the little Kent port of Ramsgate instead.

This was a deliberate snub to the larger port as a punishment for what he regarded as a gross act of disloyalty by its citizens. George and his wife Princess Caroline of Brunswick had been estranged for virtually the whole of their married lives. Forced into matrimony in April 1795, the couple had split immediately after their daughter Charlotte was born nine months later.

In short, they loathed the sight of each other, a fact that was not lost on the Great British Public who were never slow to take sides in such matters. From the very beginning of this 'marriage made in Hell' many ordinary people sided with Caroline.

Arriving in Greenwich at Easter 1795, she was greeted by an enthusiastic crowd. Now, 25 years later, the people of Dover gave her an equally rapturous reception as she returned from exile to attend the Prince of Wales' Coronation. This enraged George who regarded it as a slight against him personally. For the rest of his reign Dover would be denied the Royal Presence.

Whilst there were other departure points along England's South Coast the King had another reason to opt for Ramsgate. It was here that his lifelong friend and supporter Sir William Curtis lived at Cliff House which was situated on the cliffs above the harbour and West Pier.

Naturally, George stayed at Billy's residence the night before sailing to the Continent. No doubt the evening was a convivial one with no lack of laughter, champagne and cherry brandy.

Both as Prince Regent and King, George had not always enjoyed great popularity, so he must have wondered what sort of send off the citizens of Ramsgate would give him the next day. But his fears on this score proved groundless.

As he approached the harbour where the Royal Yacht was

NOSING THE NOB AT RAMSGATE

Not everyone showed as much respect for the King as the residents of Ramsgate. In this scurrilous cartoon, Cruikshank depicts Sir William Curtis surprising his wife and King George IV "taking coffee" at midnight in Cliff House. The *double entendre* of the illustration's title leaves the reader in no doubt that Cruikshank believed the couple were up to something else and it was certainly not having a drink! It should be pointed out that there is no evidence of Sir William Curtis being knowingly or unknowingly cuckolded by his lifetime friend George IV.

Being on the receiving end of such satire day in and out, it is hardly surprising that Billy Biscuit became exasperated with the likes of Cruikshank, Gilray and Marks.

Image © City of London, London Metropolitan Archives

moored, his carriage was flanked on both sides by crowds cheering enthusiastically. Delighted and relieved, George was determined that he would reward Ramsgate and its citizens for their loyalty.

On 27th November 1821, a letter addressed to Sir William Curtis, Chairman for The Trustees for The Improvement of The Harbour of Ramsgate was sent by Lord Sidmouth the Home Secretary:

"Sir,

I am commanded by the King to signify to you His Majesty's Pleasure that in consideration of the zeal and loyalty so eminently displayed by the inhabitants of Ramsgate when His Majesty lately embarked and disembarked at that port, the Harbour of Ramsgate be henceforth denominated a Royal Harbour ,and that the Royal Standard should be hoisted there on the day appointed for the celebration of His Majesty's Birthday, and on the anniversaries of His Majesty's Accession and Coronation."

A Committee of notable Ramsgate citizens was hastily formed to decide on a suitable memorial to mark the King's visit. Three designs were submitted by local architects.

The winning design was by John Shaw, the architect to The Harbour Trustees. It was a scaled down replica of one of the obelisks at the entrance to the ancient Egyptian city of Thebes. The total cost of the monument was £700 (=£49000 in 2010 values).

One hundred tons of Dublin Bay stone were imported for its construction. The laying of the first stone was quite an event with the honour going to The Earl of Liverpool, Lord Warden of The Cinque Ports.

Twelve English farthings, one penny, an Irish halfpenny and a Coronation medal donated by King George IV were placed in a cavity under this first stone. This probably makes the monument the earliest example of a time capsule.

In the evening, Billy Biscuit and the Lord Warden hosted a celebratory banquet for 150 distinguished citizens of Kent. Typically, Sir William Curtis ensured that the workmen who constructed the obelisk were not forgotten. He donated two sheep and four hogsheads of ale for their own feast.

It was not long before the monument earned the irreverent but affectionate nick name *"The King's Toothpick"*. It can still be seen overlooking the harbour. The inscription on it in Latin and English is as follows:

To
GEORGE THE FOURTH
King of Great Britain and Ireland
The inhabitants and visitors of Ramsgate, the Directors and Trustees of the Harbour
have erected this OBELISK
As a grateful record of His Majesty's condescension in selecting this port for His Embarkation, on 25th September, in His progress to His Kingdom of Hanover, and
his happy return
on 8th November 1821

However, this public display of loyalty probably owed as much to Ramsgate's affection for Billy Biscuit as their Monarch. A generous and kind man, Curtis was held in high esteem by the citizens of Ramsgate who called him *Father of The City*.

Some years earlier, he was also accorded the great honour of having a ship named after him. Her full title was *The Sir William Curtis Packet* and she plied her trade as a steam packet between Ramsgate and the continental port of Ostende. Sadly, after her launch, accompanied with such high hopes a few years earlier, she met a tragic end in the autumn of 1815.

When *The Sir William* left Ramsgate on the evening of Friday October 27th 1815, the fine weather gave no hint of the trouble to come. But during the crossing, the sky darkened turning the sea metal grey with a steadily increasing swell. By the time the packet reached the harbour mouth at Ostende on Sunday morning, she had missed the tide and had to wait at anchor.

When it was deemed safe to enter the harbour at seven that evening, a full scale gale was blowing with mountainous seas. Rightly or wrongly, the ship's Captain Falera delayed entry for another two hours. But this proved a fatal decision and the ship ran aground fifty yards from safety. Completely at the mercy of the storm, the packet was driven against the harbour piling. In a desperate attempt to give the passengers and crew an escape route, Captain Falera tried to fasten a rope to one of the piles. Almost immediately, a huge wave swept him overboard. By some miracle he was able to swim ashore and survived. In attempting to rescue a woman passenger, a steward was also seriously injured. By the time the vessel finally foundered, four passengers had drowned and Ramsgate had lost its prized ferry.

As an experienced ocean going yachtsman, Sir William Curtis knew only too well how treacherous the sea could be. He felt the loss of the packet ship as keenly as everyone else in the town. With characteristic generosity, he made a significant sum of money available to the families of those drowned or injured in the disaster.

But it was not only in times of adversity that Billy Biscuit looked after the interests of the port. By 1822, Ramsgate Harbour was in great need of expansion and repair. One of the main problems was that the restricted size of the harbour and the continuous threat of silting limited the size of ships to 500 tons. This denied the harbour the income from many larger merchantmen who docked at neighbouring ports such as Dover, Sandwich and Folkestone.

All that was needed for Ramsgate to prosper as a port was for engineering work to rectify these twin problems. Unfortunately, having already spent £1,500,000 the Ramsgate Harbour Trust was out of money and the necessary work was far from finished. As Chairman of the Trust, Sir William went before a Parliamentary enquiry in December 1822 to plead Ramsgate's case.

It is quite clear from contemporary reports of the proceedings that Sir William felt other ports such as Dover had unfairly elbowed Ramsgate aside when it came to lobbying for exemption from levies on larger vessels. In his characteristically pithy fashion Billy Biscuit explained the problem as he saw it: *"The fact is this, they had so powerful advocates in this House that we could not carry the Bill against them. I thought they all ought to pay, but they came upon me with their great guns, and I was obliged to yield."*

Another cause of great anger to Sir William and the citizens of Ramsgate was a levy they had to pay to the smaller harbour of Sandwich. This was because the latter possessed a Customs House and Ramsgate did not.

This meant that foreign ships docking in Ramsgate had to wait, sometimes for months, whilst the ships' agents travelled the seven miles overland to have their papers processed by the customs officers at Sandwich. On top of this inconvenience the levy of £290 had to be paid for this work. Since this was the equivalent of about £21,000 by today's values, this was no small matter.

Curtis quite clearly felt this was a stitch up. When asked by Mr Rennie the Chairman of the Parliamentary Committee whether he thought any ships docked in Ramsgate derived any benefit from this levy, Sir William replied bluntly:

"No, I believe it was a job from beginning to end."

The Sandwich Corporation were legally obliged to show The Ramsgate Trustees what *actually* happened to this £290 levy. When the Committee Chairman asked Curtis whether the Sandwich Corporation had ever done this his answer was equally blunt:

"It has never been exhibited to us: I once took the liberty of asking one of the mayors about it, I could get no answer to the question and I had no authority to press it."

Like all good prize fighters, Curtis knew when to land his knockout punch:

"I would not wish to throw any imputation on a most respectable body of men, the Corporation of Sandwich, any more than the Corporation of London."

By stating the opposite, Curtis cleverly left the Committee in no doubt what that *"most respectable body of men"* were up to. By his lights, they were nothing but a bunch of shysters pocketing the levy money for themselves.

No doubt many cups of coffee were spilled over the breakfast tables of Sandwich when these proceedings appeared in *The Times.*

As can be seen from the aerial photograph at the end of this chapter, modern Ramsgate is both a popular marina and a busy ferry port. It is fair to say this is due in no small part to Billy Biscuit championing the port's cause as the Chairman of The Harbour Trustees.

On more than one occasion this entailed putting his money where his mouth was, which he always did willingly. For example, in the harbour accounts for 1820 show he made a loan of nearly £2000 - about £120,000 in today's values.

The improvement of Ramsgate Harbour was very much Sir William's pet project. It was down to his efforts and his banking and parliamentary allies such as Peter Thellusson that it was successfully piloted through Parliament. Without such a strong champion, Royal Ramsgate could well have faded into genteel obscurity.

The residents of Ramsgate never lost their affection for the town's most celebrated resident. Indeed, when Sir William Curtis died in 1829, all the town's shops closed and a huge crowd followed the funeral cortege in a public display of respect.

Fortunately, Curtis' fine Regency residence of Cliff House has been saved from demolition and has recently been restored.

"The King's Toothpick"
The obelisk commemorating King George IV's visit to Ramsgate in 1821

ROYAL RAMSGATE

Although painted in 1854, 25 years after his death, William Powell Frith's famous painting *Ramsgate Sands, Life at the Seaside* would have been readily recognisable to Sir William Curtis. As the insets show, it also clearly depicts the Curtis residence, Cliff House on the far right. The flagpole from which the Royal Standard was flown when King George IV was visiting can also clearly be seen. The Obelisk commemorating George IV's visit to the town in 1821 and resulted in it gaining the coveted title *Royal Ramsgate* is on the left of the picture.

Aerial view of Ramsgate Harbour today
Photo courtesy of
Port of Ramsgate Authority

Ramsgate in 1795
Picture Courtesy of
The Ramsgate Society

Victorian Ramsgate
Picture Courtesy of The
Ramsgate Society

BIBLIOGRAPHY AND SOURCES

Information sources for majority of book
Wapping 1600-1800 by Derek Morris and Ken Cozens published by East London History Society 2009 ISBN 978-0-9506258-9-8
Politics, Patronage and Profit: A Case Study of Three 18th Century London Merchants by Kenneth James Cozens University of Greenwich, Greenwich Maritime Institute.
The often unfairly maligned **Wikipedia** @ http://en.wikipedia.org proved to be a very good starting point for much of the research in this book.

Chapter 5 Freemasonry
United Grand Lodge of England website @
www.ugle.org.uk

Chapter 10 - Slavery and The Wapping Merchant Network
Nick Hibbert Steele, Melbourne, Australia @
www.georgehibbert.com
Flash for Freedom by George Macdonald Fraser, Pan Books 1971 ISBN 0 330 23321 1
London, Metropolis of The Slave Trade by James A Rawley, University of Missouri Press 2007
Shipwrecks of the Revolutionary & Napoleonic Eras by Terence Grocott, Stackpole Books 1998 ISBN-10: 0811715337 ISBN-13: 978-0811715331

Chapter 11 - Politics & The 3 Rs
Nick Hibbert Steele, Melbourne, Australia @
www.georgehibbert.com

Chapter 12 - The Development of the Docks
Nick Hibbert Steele, Melbourne, Australia @
www.georgehibbert.com
Museum of London Docklands @
www.museumindocklands.org.uk

Chapter 17 - Music Lover
Phil Margolis @ www.cozio.com
John M. Broder in ***The New York Times*** dateline **19 October 2004**

Chapter 18 Czar's Dinner Service
Official website of the   City of Taganrog @
www.taganrogcity.com
Staffordshire Porcelain edited by
Geoffrey Godden published by Granada 1983
published by Collins in 1988
ISBN 0-00-215404-8
Chapter 21 - Honourable Artillery Co
   Justine Taylor, Archivist and Kirsty Bennett of **The Honourable Artillery Company**
Chapter 23 George IV Visit to Scotland
 The King's Jaunt - *George IV in Scotland* by John Prebble
Chapter 26 Royal Ramsgate
Ramsgate Maritime Museum
The Ramsgate Society website @
www.ramsgate-society.org.uk
Port of Ramsgate website @
www.ramsgatemarina.co.uk

MONETARY VALUES

It is often difficult for the modern reader to assess the true monetary value of wealth, goods and services in the Georgian period. For example, a £150 bequest in 1800 may seem like a laughably small sum until it is converted into its modern day value of approximately £10,000.

So throughout the book we have endeavoured to provide the equivalent value for the pound sterling in 2010 for the various sums of Georgian pounds shown.

To calculate this, we have used various sources including the Measuringworth website at www.measuringworth.com website.

But the relative values shown are purely an *approximate* guide to help the reader. If anyone reading this book has a better method of calculation, the authors would be delighted to hear from them.

ABOUT THE AUTHORS

John H Curtis Dolby is a direct descendant of Sir William Curtis. He was educated at St Paul's School, London and is a member of the Old Pauline Freemasonry Lodge. He is also a long standing member of The Drapers Company. He has extensive experience as businessman involved in import/export in the The Middle and Far East for fifty years. He lives in Oxfordshire, England.

Nick Brazil is an author, film maker and photographer who has made three documentaries and published two previous books books - an investigation into the supernatural called "A Journey With Ghosts" and "Cheating Death" the story of a World War Two P.O.W.

DEDICATION

This book is firstly dedicated to my Grandmother, Georgina, Lady Curtis who originally told me of the incredible life and success of Billy Biscuit and opened a new and interesting world to me as a young man.

And secondly, to my co-author Nick Brazil, whose indefatigable world wide research tracked down information wherever there was a hint of Sir William Curtis.

I have been very lucky.

John H Curtis-Dolby , Whitchurch - on -Thames, Oxfordshire
September 2010

INDEX

Abingdon, *Berks (now Oxon) UK*....38, 39,159
Abrahams, Esther..................52,53,61
Addington, Henry 44,129,135
Admiralty, The 73
Alderman's Hill 29
Allen, Nathaniel.................................63
Amati, Andrea........................101,102
Amati, Antonio & Girolamo..........102
American War of Independence. 36,49
Amsterdam....................................23,91
Antelope, HMS................................122
Angoulême, Duc d'..........................149
Archangel, *Russia*...................113,114
Armoury House, *HAC HQ*.....127,130
Attlee, Clement..................................45
Australia...........**49**,50,*51*,53-55,58-61
Austria...105
Austro-Hungarian Empire..............142
Bacolet Estate *W.Indies*...................83
Baltic (trade)..............................23,120
Bankers, *Committee for the Prevention of Frauds & Forgeries*............158
Banking.......................................**81-85**
Bank of England 26
Batavia 56
Beckwith, W. *Gunsmith* 114
Bellingham, John..................**112-116**
Black Act, The 154
Bleak House 26
Bletchingley, *Surrey, England* 136
Bligh, Capt...................................**53-54**
Blitz, The 47,78
Board Schools....................................72
Bolton, Matthew 99
Bonny, *W.Africa* 65,68

Bonnymuir *Scotland*......................141
Botany Bay, *NSW*..................49,50,52
Botany Bay Debate............................49
Boulogne, *France*...........................159
Brandreth, Josiah 134
Boroughbridge, *Yorks* 40
Bristow, John.....................................25
Britannia..41
Brodsworth Hall, *Yorks*...................29
Broke, Sir Willoughby de.............122
Bromley, C of E Primary School.....26
Bryan, The...16
Burdett, Sir Francis **40**,41,42,43,44 111
Burke's Peerage...............................98
Bushir, *Persia*...................................36
Buttersworth, Thomas...............96,*143*
Cadiz, *Spain*....................................149
Calvert, Anthony 64,69
Camden, Calvert & King (CC&K) 24,26,42,56,60,**63,65,67**,77
Camden, William & John 25,63
Canada..18,55
Canning, George............................**111**
Cape Colony, *S.Africa*.....................58
Cape Coast Castle, *W.Africa* 68
Capper St., *Walthamstow* 158
Captain General of HAC................126
Caribbean 49,**64-67**,76-78,83
Carlile, Richard 135
Cape St Vincent, Battle of...............96
Caroline *of Brunswick*.........91,92,109, 140,163
Carron *Scotland*.............................141
Castlereagh, Viscount.....*108*,**111,142 148**

Catherine the Great........................122
Chapel Royal, St James Palace.......92
Charles Ist, King of England..........126
Charles II, King of England.....11,126
Charles IX, King of France..........101
Chatham, Second Earl of *(later Lord)*. 106,111, *112,*151
China 13
Church of England......................26,**62**
Cinque Ports, *Lord Warden of*......165
City Imperial Volunteers...............132
City of London 19,24,26,73
Civil Wars, English...................87,125
Cliff House, *Ramsgate*.....................10
Clennell, Luke.................................*118*
Cleves, Anne of.................................46
Cobbett, William.............................111
Codheads, The Ancient Society of 35
Coin clipping..............................156-7
Coldbath Fields Prison, *London*......41
Coldstream Guards........................130
Comet, The.............................139,147
Commons, House of 49,**62**,65,*75,* 94,115,136,137
Commons, Father of the.................136
Cornhill 82
Cortes *Spanish Parliament* 149,152
Counterfeiting...........................156-7
Council, Guildhall Court of 126
Constable, Ann..............................**28**
Cook Islands 56,*57*
Cook, James.....................................**49**
Cope, Mr. *City Marshall*...............159
Coutts Bank 43,**84**,*85*
Coutts, Sophia 43
Coutts, Thomas 43
Cozens, Ken.........................33,64,69
Cozio Publishing 101
Crimea, *Russia* 122
Cromwell, Oliver 11,126

Cromwell, Thomas....................46-47
Cruikshank, George *108*,145,*164*
Cullands Grove, *Southgate* **29**,*32*
Cullands Grove,The (*Ship*) 68
Curtis,Ann...........................27,**28**,29
Curtis, Timothy 21
Curtis,Joseph...............11,13,14,20,21
Curtis, Lt Col William...................127
Curtis, Major P........................97-98
Curteis, John 16
Curteis, Samuel 16
Czar Alexander Ist.................**117-123**
Czar Pyotr Ist.................................117
Dalton, Hugh 45
Deal, *Kent*......................................160
Dearborn, *Michigan US*................102
Demerara, *S.America*......... 24
Dickens, Charles 26
*Dictionary of National Biography.*135
Die Jong Vrou Rebecca Maria........29
Docks, West India **76-81**
Dover, *Kent*....................119,163,167
Drapers Company ..**45-48,** 86,87,127
Drapers Hall 46,*47,48*
Dresden, Battle of.........................117
Dublin Bay stone..........................165
Duke of Danzig 56
Dundee Arms Masonic Lodge...33,34, 63,96
East India Company 22,36
East Kent Archives..........................69
Edinburgh Castle, *Scotland*..........139
Edinburgh,*Scotland*...............140,141, *143,147*
Edmonton, *London* 28
Egmont Vault, *Charlton*...............116
Eldon, Lord 109
Ellerington, William.................**59-60**
Emma *30,*69,*71,*120
....**16**,18

Enfield, *Middx* 29
Erskine, William.........................139
Ewbank, John Wilson..................*143*
Execution Dock, *Wapping*............155
Eylau, The Battle of 106
Falera, Captain...........................166
Farady, Michael 120
Father of The Commons................136
Ferdinand VII, *King of Spain*.....*148-149*
Fire, Risk of **25**
Firth of Forth *Scotland*..........139,147
Fishmonger's Company 19
Fitzailwyn, Henry Lord Mayor ..45,88
Fitzherbert, Mrs Maria 92
Fly, The 96
Flushing, *Holland* 106
Folkestone, *Kent*...........................167.
Fonblanque, John & Anthony 24
Fonnerau family 23
Forrester, *City Officer*..............159-60
Fouquier-Tinville, A-Quentin 91
Fox, Charles James MP........36,62,92
France...................23,24,40,62,73,75, 91,101,105,148,149
Freemasonry................................**33**
French Revolution.........................91
French Court.................................23
Friends, Society of 160,161
Frimley Common, *Surrey*..............154
Royal Masonic Trust for Boys and Girls..34
Gag Acts....................................133
Gainsborough, Thomas..................96
Galton, Samuel FRS......................97
Garb of Old Gaul........................144
Gascoigne, Sir Crispin....................87
Gates, Mr, *the Solicitor to the Committee of Bankers*..........................160
Geneva, *Switzerland*......................23

George III...........................63,*51,112*
GeorgeIV.......28,30,97,102, *Scottish State Visit* **139-147,** 148, *in Ramsgate* **163-170**
Gezo, King of Dahomey.................66
Gibraltar, *British Colony* **148-152**
Gilray, James.......................40, 41, 42
Giltbrook *England* 134
Glasgow *Scotland*.........................141
Gloucester, Duke of 127
Godin, Jane 23
Godleyhurst, Hundred of,*Surrey*..154
Gower, Lord Granville Leveson....113, 114
Gordon Riots...............................126
Grande Armée, (France)...............105
Gravesend 56
Great Fire of London.................86,87
Great Terror................................149
Greenland....................................**16,18**
Greenwich, *London*.....................163
Greenwich Maritime Institute........64
Grenada Exchequer Loan................83
Grenada,*West Indies* 24
Great Architect of The Universe.....33
Great Terror 91
Guardian, HMS........................**58-60**
Guildhall, Common Hall of 74
Guildhall, The ...74,86,88,89,117,*118* 119,126,156
Habeus Corpus....................41,42,135
Halifax, *Nova Scotia* 18,19
Hamilton-Dalrymple, Lady..........145
Hanover, Germany................163,166
Hardie, Andrew...........................141
Harding, Lt Frederick 122
Hart, George...............................156
Hawksbee, Francis........................45
Haydn, Franz Joseph 102

Henry VIII..............................46,125
Henry Ford Museum, *US*..............102
Hickey, William............................35
Hibbert, George 23
Horsham Jail, Sussex England......133
Holman, Francis 96
Holyroodhouse, *Edinburgh*...140,145, *146*
Holy Land, *M.East*.........................87
Honourable Artillery Company 28, **125-130**
Hood, Admiral 36
Hotham, Baron 153
Huggins, William J 96
Huguenot(s).................................23
Hunton, Joseph **157-162**
Iberia..105
India 17
International Bankers, Guild of 87
Inuit 18
Ipswich Journal...........................157
Isfahan, *Persia*..............................36
Jackson, Sir George.......................50
Jamaica 24
James Watt, The....................139,147
Jefferson, Thomas 65
Jeffreys, Judge..............................45
Jenkins, Capt Robert 49
Jenkins Ear, War of.........................49
Jerusalem Sols, Order of 36
Jew(s).....................................62,*85*
Johnston, Lt George..................53,54
Kensington Palace, *London*..........132
Kent (*County*) *England*.........27,28,30, 136,160,163,165
Keppel, Viscount..........................45
King's Toothpick, The.............165,*169*
Knights Templar 35
Kurnell Peninsula, *NSW*................50
Labrador Sea *Canada*....................18

Lady Juliana........................52,58,59
Lady Penrhyn.................**50**,*51*,53 -56
Lawrence, Sir Thomas..............96,97
Lear, George 23
Lear, Mary Anne 23
Leeds, *Yorks* 159
Legge,Thomas, Lord Mayor...........88
Leigh St.,*Manchester* 157
Leipzig, Battle of.........................117
Leith Harbour *Scotland* *143*
Leyton, *Essex* (St Mary's Church)..23
Leverton, Thomas 29
Liverpool, City of 68,*71*,112,114
Liverpool, Earl of........................165
Liverpool, Lord 134,135,141
Liverymen's Common Hall 88
Lloyds Coffee House...............50,113
Lombard St, *City* 82,84
London......................................19,23
Longastre, L de 28,**97-99**,*100*
Longbows,Crossbows & Handguns, Guild of 125
Lord Mayor................28,45,46,74,**86** -92,94,98,101,125,131,156
Lords, House of 26
Los Angeles Philharmonic Orchestra **102-103**
Lottery (slave ship)........................24
Louis XIV, *King of France* 23
Lubbock, Forster & Co...................84
Luddites......................................129
Lumsden, James 35
Lunar Society 97
Lyndhurst, *Hants*..........................98
MacDonell, Alastair R 140,144
MacDougall, Captain Ewan..........140
Mack, General............................105
Madrid.......................................149
Madrid, Royal Palace Collection..102
Magna Carta 88

Major, John MP for Scarborough...21
Malaria...107
Maldon, *Surrey, England*.................38
Manchester *England*.......133,134,157
Manchester Times..........................135
Mansfield, Lord Chief Justice.......116
Mansion House.................87,88,90,98
March of the Blanketeers..............133
Margolis, Phil...................................101
Mayfair, *London*...............................92
Methodists..62
Metternich, Prince 142
Midlands, The *England*..............13,99
Midlothian Yeomanry......................140
Milligan, Robert.........................**76-81**
"Middlesex Election 1804"...............40
Midhurst, Sussex 26
Mithras 35
Moline, Sparks.................................162
Monarchy, Restoration of.........11,126
Morning Chronicle, The 160
Morning Post, The..........................159
Museum of London Docklands .*57,68*
78,79
Music **101-104**
Nadar Afsah Shah of Persia...**35**,36,*37*
Naples, *Italy*.............................151,152
Napoleon Bonaparte ...96,98,105,117
Napoleonic Wars.........11,38,129,140,
150
Nelson, Horatio..................45,36,127
Neptune......................................**58-60**
Newgate Prison, *London*..........53,161
New Model Army............................126
New York *US* 159,160
New York Times 102
New Zealand......................................56
Nootka Sound & Convention..........**55**
North America **16**,17,20,49
Northampton, *England*..................109
North Atlantic....................................17
North Sea........................105,106,120
Nottingham 11
Nottingham (*ship*)............................96
Nova Scotia.........................**16**,17,18
"Nova Scotia" baking method..........19
Old Bailey.............................52,53,160
Oldenburg, Duchess of 119
Oliver, William................................134
Oxford, *England*............................119
Paris, *France* 23
Parker, Fell 63
Park Lane, *London*..........................92
Park, Mr Justice..............................160
Parliament, Reform of 41
Penrhyn Island..........................**56**,*57*
Pentrich Uprising 134
Persia...35
Perceval, Spencer MP PM.....**109-116**
Peter the Great 122
Peterloo Massacre 43,**134-135**
Philpot Lane, City of London 23
Phillip, Capt Arthur..................50, *51*
Pichegru, General............................91
Pitt Government 40,44
Pitt, Moses..63
Pitt, William 36,41
Plaistow Lodge, *Bromley*, ...**26**,*27*,29
Plymouth, *Devon*...........................159
Political Register, The 111
Pool of London 13
Pope Pius V....................................101
Port Jackson, *NSW*...........50,55,58-60
Portland, Lord 111
Portsmouth, *Hants*........................159
Prince Regent, The....37,55,86,92,109
114,157,132,133,135,136,163
Prospect of Whitby Pub..................11
Prussia, *Germany*....................105,148
Prussia, King of 117,*118*

Quaker(s).....................13,62,**158-161**
Radical War, The 141
Ramsgate, *Kent*.........10,28,30,33,163,
Ramsgate Harbour Trust............**167-9**
Rangeston, William......................151
Ratcliff Wharf Area 25
Red Lyon Street, Wapping...............33
Regalia of Scotland......................140
Reynolds, Sir Joshua.....................96
Rhine, River *Germany* 105
Richard the Lionheart......................87
Riego, Col. Rafael 148-149
Riou, Lt Edward 58
Robarts, Curtis, Were, Hornyold, Berwick & Co 82
Robinson, Duncan 153
Robinson,Rev.*of Thurstonland*.....157
Royal Charlotte (*slave ship*)............64
Royal Charter 45
Royal George, The 139,*143,*147
Royal Institution of Gt Britain....120,122
Royal Navy............9,22,24,66,98,120
Royal Society, The......................45,97
Rum Rebellion *NSW*......................53
Russell, Matthew MP.....................136
Russia..........61,112-117,120,122,148
Sandwich, *Kent* **167-8**
Salomon, J.P................................102
Scandinavia....................................11
Scarborough 58-59
Scotland.............................33, 36,148
Scotland, Royal Bank of.................84
Scotland, *Royal Visit to* **139-147**
Scott, Sir Walter............139,140,142, 144,147
Seaford, Sussex 38
Severs,Capt William Cropton..50,**53-56**
Sea biscuits...............9,13,17,22,69,82
Shaw, John....................................165

Sicily, *Italy*...................................151
Sidmouth, Lord...............125,126,129, **130-135,**165
Sierra Leone, *W.Africa* 69,*70*
Sierra Leone, *Mixed Commission Court of* 69
Sirius,HMS 50
Sir William Curtis Packet............166
Slane Castle *N.Ireland*.................142
Slave Coast, *W. Africa* 65-71
Slave galleys..................................23
Slavery Abolition Act 1833 68
Slavery & Slave Trade..36,**62-68,**109
Slave Trade Act.............................64
Soluere..113
Sothebys....................................97,98
South America 24
South Bank (*of London*) 19
South Dakota, Nat Museum of 101
Soviet Authorities.........................122
Spa Fields, *Islington*..............129,130
Spa Fields Riots.................... 131,133
Spanish Court..............................102
Spenceans....................................129
Spithead, *S.England* 58,119,160
Springfield 16
Steele, Nick Hibbert....................67,69
Sting Ray Bay *NSW*......................49
Stirling *Scotland* 141
St George, Guild of 125
St Petersburg, *Russia* 113,120,122 *124*
St Jean Prison, Marseilles, *France* 91
St Peter's Field, *Manchester*.........134
Stow, John 11
Stradivari(us)........................102,103
Stray,John.......................................63
Suffolk (County) 21
Surprise...58
Sussex (County) *England*...............26

Sussex, Duke of 132
Sweden......................................105
Sydney Cove *NSW* 50,*51*,53
Taganrog,*Crimea, Russia* 122,*123*
Tahiti, *Polynesia*........................55-56
Tartan Pageant, The 142
Tenterden, *Kent*........................28,29,
Territorial Army.....................126,132
Test & Corporation Acts.................62
Texel, *Holland* 91
Thames, River 29, 89
Thellusson,Peter Isaac Sr......23,24,26
Thellusson,Peter Isaac Jr.....24,26
Thellusson Wills Case 26
Thistlewood, Arthur........129,130,131, 133
Thornton, Godfrey...........................23
Three Sisters(slave ship)..................25
*Three Good Friends (*slave ship*)*...........64
Three Rs, The................................72
Throgmorton St ,*City* 46,47
Thurstonland,*Huddersfield, UK*....157
Times, The................119,151,153,154, 160,168
Tinian *Pacific Ocean*......................56
Titanic, The 18
Tongarava (*Penrhyn Island*).*P.O*....56
Tory Party & MPs.....26,**62**,64,86,109
Tower of London.........43,*80*,111,*112*, 129,130,159
Townend, Peter...............................98
Town of Ramsgate, The., PH........11,12,
Trafalgar, Battle of 127,*150*
Traill, Donald.............................**59,60**
Trained bands...............................125
Trocadero Fort , *Cadiz Spain* 149
True Highlanders, *Society of* 140
Ulm, *Bavaria*................................105
Unlawful Societies Act 36
Van Brienen, Solomon..................113

Vendeneyvers 23
Verona, Congress & Treaty of 141, 142, 148
Vienna, Treaty of..........................148
Viotti, Giovanni Battista........101-102
Waddenzee, *Holland*......................91
Wagram, Battle of 106
Walker, "Irish Mick".....................153
Walker, James...............................*112*
Walcheren Expedition.....**105-107**,109, 151
Walcheren Fever 107
Wales, Prince of 28,36
Walthamstow, *Middx* 158
Wapping..**11**,14,18,19,20,24,25,33,34 42
Wapping Merchants Network ... 23,24
War, First World...........................132
War, Second World................122,132
War, South African.......................132
Waterloo, Battle of 83,135
Waverley......................................142
Weasel HMS................................151
Wedderburn, Robert......................135
Wedderburns..................................56
Wedgewood, John..........................99
Weevils 17,22
Wellesley, Marquis of...................114
Wellington, Duke of 105,114, 148
West Africa..............................**64-67**
West End (of London)....................19
West Indian Plantations 64
West Indies Trade.......24,**62-69**,*71*,77, 83
Westminster 42
Whig Party & MPs.........45,62,92,136
White Hart, The PH 136
White House, *Washington US* 65
White Sea, *Russia* 113
Whydah, *W.Africa* 65

Wilberforce, William MP ...**64,68**,109
Wilkins, Edward............................159
Willem V..91
Wokingham Blacks........................154
Woodford, Ann............................... 23
Woodford, Matthew..23/2 (*family*).26
Wood, Thomas & Elizabeth..........156
Yarmouth Great, *Suffolk*................158
York (City) *England*.................13,129
York, Duke of...............................126